Summertime
Book 4

Mary Underwood

PHOENIX
ELT

incorporating
PRENTICE HALL MACMILLAN

New York London Toronto Sydney Tokyo Singapore

© Mary Underwood 1994

This edition first published 1995 by Phoenix ELT
Campus 400, Spring Way
Maylands Avenue, Hemel Hempstead
Hertfordshire, HP2 7EZ

A division of Prentice Hall International

© International Book Distributors Ltd

All rights reserved. No part, copy or transmission of this publication may be made without written permission or in accordance with provisions of the Copyright, Designs and Patents Act 1988, or under the terms of any licence permitting limited copying issued by the Copyright Licensing Agency, 90 Tottenham Court Road, London W1P 9HE.

Typeset in Garamond and Gill Sans Condensed

Produced by **AMR**

Illustrations by Jane Jones, Kareen Taylerson, Charles Whelon

Printed and bound Malta by Interprint Limited

British Library Cataloguing in Publication Data
A catalogue record for this book is available from The British Library

ISBN 013-459587-4

5 4 3 2 1
99 98 97 96 95

The author and publisher would like to thank the following photographic sources:

Colorsport p.61 (1); Greg Evans International p.16 (x2), p.48; Mary Evans Picture Library p.3 (x2), p. 36, p.78; Hulton Deutsch Collection Ltd p.20, p.21; John Miller/Personal Computer World p.82; John H. Paul Photography p. 6; Popperfoto Ltd p.61 (r), p.65 (x2), p.66, p.71 (t, m); Rex Features Ltd p.24, p.60; Syndication International Ltd p.71 (tl, tr); The Channel Tunnel Group Ltd p.70(x3).

The author and publisher also wish to thank the following who have kindly given permission for the use of copyright material:

Extract from *The Puffin Book of Heroic Failures* by Stephen Pile, published by Penguin Books (pages 2, 3)

Extract from the *Daily Mail* October 20 1993, reproduced by permission of Solo Syndication (pages 6, 7)

Extracts from *The Colour Eye* by Robert Cumming, published by BBC Books, reprinted by permission of the Peters Fraser & Dunlop Group Ltd (pages 8, 9, 11)

Extracts from *Agatha Christie – the woman and her mysteries* by Gillian Gill, published by Robson Books Ltd (pages 20, 21, 24)

Extract from *Agatha Christie, An Autobiography*, published by Fontana/Collins (page 25)

Extract from *Frankenstein* by Mary Shelley, simplified version by Patrick Nobles, reproduced by permission of Oxford University Press (page 36)

Extract from *Frankenstein* by Mary Shelley, published by Clio Press Ltd (page 37)

Poem *Coming From Kansas* by Myra Cohn Livingstone, from 'Worlds I know', published by Macmillan Inc. (page 54)

Extract from *Matilda* by Roald Dahl, published by Penguin Books Ltd (page 55)

Extract from *The Return of Heroic Failures* by Stephen Pile, published by Penguin Books Ltd (page 56)

Extract from *The Complete How to Handle Grown-ups* by Jim and Duncan Eldridge, published by Red Fox (page 58)

Extracts from *The Times* May 1 1993, reproduced by permission of © Times Newspapers Ltd (pages 60, 61)

Extract from *The Daily Telegraph* January 8 1994, *The Sunday Telegraph* April 4 1993, *The Daily Telegraph* December 11 1993, *The Sunday Telegraph* October 31 1993, reproduced by permission of Ewan McNaughton Associates (pages 60, 61, 62, 64, 65)

The Channel Tunnel Group Ltd for information used in Unit 12 (pages 66, 67, 68, 69, 70, 71)

Extract from *The Times Higher Education Supplement* October 29 1993, reproduced by permission of © Times Newspapers Ltd (page 75)

Extract from *The Puffin Book of Heroic Failures* by Stephen Pile, published by Penguin Books (page 80)

Extract used in Unit 14 reproduced by permission of *Dave's Disk Doctor Service Ltd* (page 81)

Extract from *Personal Computer World* February 1994 (page 84)

Every effort has been made to trace all the copyright holders but if any have been inadvertently overlooked, the publishers will be pleased to make the necessary arrangement at the first opportunity.

Contents

1	What bad luck!	2
2	What's your favourite colour?	8
3	'The Lion'	14
4	Agatha Christie's greatest mystery	20
5	Interesting numbers	26
6	A part-time job	30
7	Frankenstein's monster	36
8	Well done!	42
9	Staying at the Wessex	48
10	Visitors	54
11	Nasty moments in sport	60
12	The Channel Tunnel	66
13	Is it a fake?	72
14	The world of computers	78
15	Person to person	84

1 What bad luck!

Bad luck   can strike   at any time!

1a Take a very quick look at the paragraph below. It's the beginning of a story. Decide:

1. what the story is about. _____
2. who it is about. _____
3. when it happened. _____

> In 1932, the Olympic Games were held in Los Angeles. One of the big races was expected to be the 3,000 metres steeplechase in which a Finnish athlete called Volmari Iso-Hollo was hoping to break the world record. He went into the lead from the very first lap and from then on no-one at all could catch him.

1b Do you think he broke the world record? _____

What kind of bad luck do you think he had? _____

1c Read the whole story on the opposite page and then write a sentence here explaining what all the runners had to do and why.

_____
_____

1d Choose headings from this list for the four paragraphs in the story and write one of them above each paragraph.

> **Iso-Hollo's great run**   **The last lap?**
> **On target for the record**   **What a record!**
> **The infamous 3,000 metres steeplechase** **Confusion all round**
> **The incompetent official**   **An extra lap**

1e Now use another title from the list in 1d as the title for the whole story.

In 1932, the Olympic Games were held in Los Angeles. One of the big races was expected to be the 3,000 metres steeplechase in which a Finnish athlete called Volmari Iso-Hollo was hoping to break the world record. He went into the lead from the very first lap and from then on no-one at all could catch him. Lap after lap, he was on target for the record. The crowd became more and more excited and roared him on, particularly as he approached the final lap.

But as Iso-Hollo came up to the bell for the last lap, the official was looking the other way, watching the decathlon pole vault, and he failed to ring the bell. Iso-Hollo ran on, unsure about how many laps remained. The crowd was confused and the shouting gave way to angry muttering.

After a further lap, the official, who had now turned back to his duties, rang the bell to indicate that the runners had one more lap to complete. Iso-Hollo went on, still in the lead, and finally won the race.

Unfortunately, the competitors had all run an extra lap – an extra 400 metres – and the time for the race was given as 10 minutes 33.4 seconds – the slowest time ever for an Olympic 3,000 metres steeplechase. It was a record but not the one Iso-Hollo wanted!

(It was later discovered that the official in charge of counting the laps had been taken ill and it was a substitute who had made the mistake.)

1f   Circle two words which are used in the story to describe how the crowd felt. Write two sentences explaining why they felt like this.

   1 _____
     _____
   2 _____
     _____

1g   Find these phrases in the story and write a brief explanation of each one.

   1 to break the world record _____
   2 He went into the lead _____
   3 roared him on _____
   4 came up to the bell _____

3

2a Now read this (true) story about a man who wanted to repair his roof. As you read on, you will need to choose the correct word from each box. Underline the word you choose.

How unlucky can you be?

A man who was repairing the roof of his house after a storm slipped and fell off the roof. Although it was a long way to the ground, he was quite lucky – he only suffered a broken leg and some bruises. His wife called an ambulance and he was taken to hospital where they put his leg in plaster and gave him a pair of crutches to use.

'I think you should try walking with the crutches before you go home,' said the nurse. 'Some people find them hard to get used to.' So the man set off down the corridor using the crutches.

'No problem,' he said, but the nurse was too far away to hear him clearly. 'Pardon?' she replied. The man turned his head to repeat his comment, but just at that moment one of the crutches slipped and he fell to the ground, pinning his hand underneath him and breaking one of his fingers.

Very soon, his finger was attended to and his hand was put in plaster. 'Sit here and don't move until I tell you,' said the nurse, 'I'll get an ambulance to take you home.'

The man sat | to wait / waiting / waited | for over an hour. Eventually, he | decided / expected / chose | that he wouldn't wait any longer.

He lived quite | closed / closely / close | to the hospital and he was | definite / sure / clear | he could get home on his crutches. So he set

off, taking | care / caring / carefully | not to turn round as he went down the corridor, out of the hospital and into the street.

As he turned the corner into his road, he saw a neighbour painting the upstairs windows of his house. 'Whatever's happened to you?' shouted the neighbour, but the man couldn't hear. 'What did you say,' asked the man. 'I'll come down,' said the friend. But just as he started to move down the ladder, his paint-pot fell and hit the man on the ground on the head. The man woke up back in the hospital he'd just left. He had to have seven stitches in his head.

2b Put 'Yes' beside the things you can tell for sure from the story in 2a and 'No' beside the ones you can't be sure about. For each 'Yes,' write down the part of the story which gives you the information.

   1 whether the man finished repairing his roof _____
   2 what injuries he received when he fell off his roof _____
   3 whether crutches are easy to use _____
   4 which finger the man broke _____
   5 how many parts of the man were in plaster when he left the hospital
      _____
   6 why the neighbour started to come down his ladder _____
   7 who put the seven stitches in the man's head _____

2c Find these parts of the story in 2a and answer the questions.

   1 '... they put his leg in plaster ... .' Who put his leg in plaster?
      _____
   2 'Some people find them hard to get used to.' Find what hard to get used to?
      _____
   3 'The man turned his head to repeat his comment' Which comment?
      _____
   4 '... painting the upstairs windows of his house.' Whose house?
      _____
   5 '... his paint-pot fell ... .' Whose paint-pot fell?
      _____

2d What words are used in the story in 2a to connect the two parts of these sentences?

   1 'No problem,' he said _____ the nurse was too far away to hear him.
   2 Very soon, his finger was attended to _____ his hand was put in plaster.
   3 So he set off, taking care not to turn round _____ he went down the corridor ... .
   4 'Whatever's happened to you?' shouted the neighbour _____ the man couldn't hear.

2e The nurse who looked after him on his first visit to the hospital came into the room where he was having the stitches put in his head. What do you think she said to him?

      _____
      _____

5

3a Use your dictionary to look up the words which are underlined in these sentences and make a note about what each one means.

1 The work was done without a single <u>hitch</u>.
2 It was a long <u>hike</u>.
3 Why don't you <u>hitch-hike</u> to Budapest?

3b Now look at these headlines. They are all about the same news story. Write one short sentence describing what the news item might be about.

HIKER'S UNLUCKY HITCH

HITCH FOR A HIKER

LOST IN THE MOUNTAINS

_____
_____
_____

3c Read the first part of the newspaper report and find out:

1 who the story is about. _____
2 what he got a lift on. _____
3 how long he spent on it. _____

TEN HOURS IN CHAIRLIFT TRAP FOR PEAK WALKER WHO TRIED TO GET DOWN THE EASY WAY

When hillwalker Terence Magee saw an empty chairlift heading down the mountainside, he gave in to temptation and jumped aboard.

But seconds later, it juddered to a halt. And instead of getting a quick ride back to his car, he spent ten hours dangling in mid-air in the darkness and bitter cold.

As he swayed helplessly in the icy winds and gathering dusk 50ft above the Aviemore slopes in the Highlands, his cries went unheard.

3d Underline the words in the text in 3c which could be replaced by each of the following words. Write the 'new' words in the margin opposite each one.

1 going down
2 could not resist
3 got on it
4 shook
5 hanging
6 severe
7 moved from side to side
8 approaching darkness
9 shouts

3e Now read the details about how it happened.

The 45-year old RAF sergeant was at 2,000ft, heading down to the car park on Cairn Gorm, when he hitched his ill-fated ride on the chairlift at 4.15pm. The machinery had been switched on temporarily because technicians at the base station were working on it. But seconds after Mr Magee boarded, it was switched off again – leaving him dangling.

6

3f Which of these sentences explains why Mr Magee was left hanging in the air?

1. Mr Magee hadn't noticed the time and the chairlift was switched off at 4.15pm.
2. The machinery had been switched off temporarily so that some technicians could repair it and then it was switched on again.
3. The machinery had been switched on temporarily to check whether it was working and then it was switched off again.
4. The machinery was switched off at the base station just when Mr Magee got on the chairlift at the top of the mountain.

3g At 10.00 pm, Mr Magee's wife reported to the police that her husband had not come home. Here is the part of the report about how Mr Magee was found and finally rescued.

> The mountain rescue team set out and finally heard his shouts and whistles coming from the darkness at about 1.30 am. After firing a flare, they found him half an hour later.
> However, Mr Magee's ordeal was still not over. Because the chairlift could not be started, a rope ladder had to be hooked on to his chair and he scrambled down it – jumping the final 15ft to the ground. 'Before we got him down we were able to throw him a flask with a hot drink in it,' said Mr Allen. 'He was unhurt but very embarrassed and very cold. He was also very lucky. The temperature had improved and it was only just freezing overnight. The previous night it was –6°C.'

3h Afterwards, Mr Magee wrote to tell his brother about his ordeal. Complete this part of his letter, using information from the newspaper report.

> At about ¹_____, I thought I could hear people. Suddenly they ²_____ and the whole area was lit up. Someone shouted something and I realized they'd seen me. I was so relieved, but, of course, the next problem was how to ³_____. They couldn't start the ⁴_____ so they told me they'd have to get me down with a ⁵_____. While they were sorting that out, somebody managed to ⁶_____. Eventually they got me down the ladder. I was feeling ⁷_____ and very ⁸_____. They told me I was very ⁹_____. The temperature was only about ¹⁰_____ that night. (The night before it had been ¹¹_____!)

Think of at least five unlucky things that could happen to each of the people below. Then ask your friends for their ideas. Are they better than yours?

a teenager cycling to a football match

a man carrying lots of shopping home

a woman running to catch a bus

2 What's your favourite colour?

In 1941, a man called Hans Eysenck collected the data from all the colour preference tests he could find and put the results into the 'universal order of colour'. The tests were all based on the colours of the spectrum, with purple added. Eysenck found that people's colour preferences were: 1 blue; 2 red; 3 green; 4 purple; 5 yellow; 6 orange. Does your choice agree with this order? Do you know why you like a particular colour more than any others?

1a Look at this chart and find out all you can about your favourite colour.

	Symbolic meanings	Different meanings in different cultures
Red	fire and passion energy and strength evil and disaster (the colour of the devil)	In ancient Egypt – the colour of the sun god Ra. In Roman mythology – the colour of Mars, the god of War In China – the marriage colour For Amercian Indians – disaster
Orange	warmth fruit and flowers sunset	Buddhist monks wear it as a sign of humility In China and Japan – the colour of love and happiness
Yellow	the sun cowardice	In ancient Greece – fire and the sun For Hindus – life and truth; the marriage colour For the Chinese – the earth colour
Green	spring nature hope	For the Chinese – wood For Leonardo da Vinci – water In ancient Greece – the colour of Venus, goddess of love The sacred colour of Islam
Blue	the sky the sea space and depth authority sincerity	For Christians – the colour of the Virgin Mary In Roman mythology – the colour of Mercury, the winged messenger of the Gods
Purple/Violet	knowledge holiness sorrow old age	Kings and Emperors often wear purple The Byzantine royal family wrapped their babies in purple clothes For Christians – worn by priests at baptisms, and during the period before Easter and Christmas
Black		

The psychology of the colours

- the second most favoured colour
- young children often like red best but as teenagers they change and like blue best
- when people are exposed to red, their bodies react – their blood pressure rises, they breathe more quickly and they feel hotter

- lovers of orange are often cheerful and talkative, they like company and plenty of activity
- used in factories to show things which are extremely dangerous (e.g. hot pipes, electric wires, saws)

- chosen by people who are intelligent, who like new ideas, who have great hopes
- well liked by mentally handicapped people
- avoided by people who are suspicious
- used in industry to make people look carefully (e.g. low doors, moving equipment)

- liked by people who are well-balanced and civilised
- used to refer to someone who is inexperienced
- liking blue-green shows self-centredness
- a good colour for meditation and thought

- the most popular favourite colour
- people who like blue are conservative, clever and successful
- lovers of blue like order and peace
- not liking blue shows anxiety and a sense of failure
- when exposed to blue, people's blood pressure goes down and they become calm

- chosen by people who are sensitive and who like the arts, music and ballet
- lovers of purple are temperamental
- people who dislike violet avoid close relationships

1b Write down:

1 the most well-known symbolic meaning of your favourite colour.

    _____

2 the most interesting meaning of your favourite colour in another culture.

    _____

3 the most relevant statement to you in the 'psychology of the colours' section of your favourite colour.

    _____

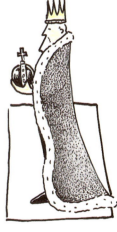

1c Use the chart to find the colours for these kinds of people:

   1 people who like order and peace _____
   2 people who like new ideas _____
   3 people who like music _____
   4 people who are cheerful _____
   5 people who are well-balanced _____
   6 people who are temperamental _____
   7 people who like company _____
   8 people who are clever and successful _____

1d Which colour symbolises:

   1 the sea? _____   4 hope? _____
   2 evil? _____   5 energy? _____
   3 sorrow? _____

1e Write down the abstract noun which is related to each of these adjectives.
    All the abstract nouns you need are in the first column of the chart on pages 8 and 9.

   1 strong *strength* _____   6 cowardly _____
   2 spacious _____   7 deep _____
   3 hopeful _____   8 energetic _____
   4 holy _____   9 sincere _____
   5 warm _____   10 passionate _____

1f Complete these statements, using information from the second column in the chart.

   1 In Japan, _____ is the colour of love.
   2 For Hindus, the colour for weddings is _____ but in China it's _____ .
   3 For American Indians, _____ symbolises disaster.
   4 Christian priests often wear _____ for baptisms.
   5 _____ is the sacred colour of Islam.

1g Complete the section for 'black' at the bottom of the chart on pages 8 and 9, using any information or ideas you have.

2a Here is some advice from an expert about the colours to paint different rooms. If you followed the advice, what colour would you paint each of the rooms listed below the text?

> If you want to make a room look smaller and warmer, use red. An experiment conducted in Norway showed that if you put people in red or blue rooms where the temperature is exactly the same they will turn the heating up four degrees higher in the blue room than in the red room. And red is good for restaurants, especially fast food restaurants. This is because people eat more quickly when they are in a red room and so the restaurant can do more business.
>
> Pink is good for bedrooms, because it has a calming effect. And red and yellow are good in the hall because they make people feel welcome.
>
> Blue is suitable in places where you want people to feel relaxed. It also seems to 'push the walls back', so, if you want to make a room look bigger, try painting it blue.
>
> Green is often said to be the most calming colour of all and is used in lots of hospitals. The 'green room' is used to describe the room where actors wait before they go on to the stage.
>
> Some people say that yellow is stressful. They believe that this is why mentally disturbed people use it so much in their paintings. Other people say that it is good to use in a study, where we want the mind to be active and busy. Many people use yellow in kitchens and bathrooms to cheer themselves up.

1 a kitchen _____
2 a bedroom _____
3 a hall _____
4 a hospital ward _____
5 a restaurant _____

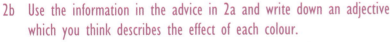

2b Use the information in the advice in 2a and write down an adjective which you think describes the effect of each colour.

1 red _____
2 pink _____
3 blue _____
4 green _____
5 yellow _____

2c What colours are the rooms in your home painted? Would you like any of them to be a different colour? If so, what colour? Complete this chart.

	present colour	change? Yes/No	new colour
entrance hall			
kitchen			
bathroom			
my bedroom			
the room where we eat			
the room where we sit and watch TV			
(other rooms)			

3a Psychologists say that the colour of people's cars tells you something about the people. Read this newspaper article.

COLOURS AND CAR DRIVERS

Next time you get stuck behind a slow driver, look at the colour of his car. It'll probably be green. American researchers have found that green cars are chosen by stubborn drivers who won't get out of the way for anybody. They also criticise other drivers for the way they drive.

Blue is the colour chosen by the relaxed motorist. He is unlikely to get angry with other drivers and will almost certainly stop and let you pull out of a side road.

Black was the only colour available when cars were first sold. There is a famous remark which

The research also showed that bright red cars are usually driven by extroverts who hate being overtaken. And, it is claimed, yellow cars are always in a hurry. Drivers of yellow cars won't wait in a traffic jam; they will turn off the road and try to find an alternative route.

Henry Ford, the producer of the first motor cars, is supposed to have made when somebody asked about what colour car they could have: '... any colour so long as it's black'. Now, black has become a popular colour in some countries because it is 'different' and rare.

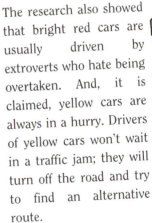

3b Which colours does the text in 3a tell you about?

_____   _____   _____

_____   _____

3c Find the words in the text in 3a which tell you:

1 that drivers of green cars talk about other drivers.

2 that the writer of the article has evidence about the drivers of red cars.

3 that you won't see many yellow cars in a traffic jam.

4 that drivers of blue cars don't lose their tempers.

5 that nobody is certain whether Henry Ford ever did say the famous line about black cars.

3d Underline a sentence in 'Colours and car drivers' where the writer is telling you:

1 something that is probably true.
2 that he is not positive that the fact is 100% true.
3 that he is fairly sure that the driver will behave in the way he describes.
4 that he is reporting something which is well-known but not guaranteed to be true.

Think of five car drivers you know and write their names in Column 1 of the chart. In Column 2, write the colour of their cars. In Column 3, write down whether you think that particular colour is suitable for each person, using the information from the text in 3a. If you write 'No' in Column 3, write the colour you think they should have in Column 4 and add the reason why.

Col 1	Col 2	Col 3	Col 4

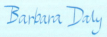

'The Lion'

1a Take a quick look at this title page from a magazine and write down:

1 what kind of magazine it is.

2 the name of the school.

3 the name of the head teacher.

4 the title of the section which begins on page 16.

5 how many sections there are in the magazine.

The magazine of Greylands Secondary School

HEAD LINES

With the recent opening of the Mary Bell Music Rooms, our five-year building programme was completed. It is hard to imagine life without the noise and dust we have had to put up with for so long! The patience of staff and students during this difficult period has been rewarded with the wonderful new rooms and facilities which are now in full use.

Former students who come to visit the school find it almost unrecognisable. 'Where's the window Peter smashed with his football?' asks one. 'The chemistry lab was much smaller than this when I was at school' remarks another. 'What's happened to the library? Where's it gone?' asks a third. But the school is more – much more – than its buildings and all those who come back can still find the happy, caring atmosphere which they remember from their own schooldays.

This year the school has had more successes than ever. Exam results were exceptional. Our sports teams won major trophies. More students have taken part in music and drama activities. Twice as many students as last year have been on school trips, some as far away as the Arctic Circle.

I am proud of our achievements and congratulate all those involved.

Barbara Daly

Head Teacher

CONTENTS

Contents list	1
Head Lines	1
News and Comment	2
Staff Changes	3
Opening of the Mary Bell Music Rooms	6
Music Notes	7
Sports Section	11
Drama	15
Trips Abroad	16
Canal Expedition	20
School Clubs	21
Words and Pictures	22

1b What does the Head Teacher say:

   1 is now completed?
   _____

   2 is hard to imagine?
   _____

   3 are now in full use?
   _____

   4 is more than its buildings?
   _____

   5 were exceptional?
   _____

   6 the school sports teams have won?
   _____

1c Go through the 'Head Lines' again and look at each paragraph in turn.

   Put **1** beside a sentence in the first paragraph where the writer talks about the past.

   Put **2** beside a sentence in the second paragraph where the writer reports what someone else has said.

   Put **3** beside a sentence in the third paragraph where the writer talks about events which have finished.

1d Use the Contents List in 1a and decide which section of *The Lion* you should turn to if you want to find out:

   1 something about the new teachers.
   _____

   2 who organised the trip to the Arctic Circle.
   _____

   3 how many matches the soccer team won.
   _____

   4 who went to the opening of the new Music Rooms.
   _____

   5 whether any of your friends have written any poetry for the school magazine.
   _____

2a Read this part of 'Staff Changes' and complete the notes about Mr Jessop and Mrs Howard.

The Lion

WELCOME

In September, we welcomed **Mr Colin Jessop** to the teaching staff. Mr Jessop, an Oxford graduate, has replaced Mr Charles Porter as Head of Maths. Mr Jessop comes to us from the post of Head of Maths at Stratford School, where he played a large part in the development of Computing Studies. He is a keen swimmer and walker and has spent much of his leisure time on these hobbies. He is also a qualified meteorologist and, under his guidance, the Meteorology Club at Stratford School has become famous for its weather forecasts.

Mrs Dorothy Howard will join us in January. She is a native of Scotland, with a degree in Chemistry from Edinburgh University. After completing a higher degree, Mrs Howard worked in industry for twelve years before training to become a teacher. She has been teaching Chemistry and Biology at New Cross School for the past three years and now joins our Chemistry department, in which she will have special responsibility for the new junior syllabus. Mrs Howard's hobbies are sailing and music. She is an accomplished trumpet player and has promised to take an active part in the school orchestra.

Mr Jessop

Joined the staff in [1]_____ as [2]_____

University attended: [3]_____

Previous appointment: [4]_____

School extra-curricula activities: [5]_____

Hobbies: [6]_____

Mrs Howard

Joined the staff in [1]_____ as [2]_____

University attended: [3]_____

Previous appointment: [4]_____

School extra-curricula activities: [5]_____

Hobbies: [6]_____

2b What do you think is the most interesting thing about:

1   Mr Jessop? _____

2   Mrs Howard? _____

3a Read this brief report about the opening of the Mary Bell Music Rooms.

The Lion

The opening of the new music rooms on 26 May was a happy occasion for the school. We were greatly honoured by the presence of Professor Mary Bell, the eminent violinist, after whom the music rooms have been named. Although the whole programme had to be put back by an hour due to the unforeseen delay in Professor Bell's arrival, everyone who came to the ceremony, and attended the concert which followed, agreed that it was a most enjoyable evening.

3b Find three adjectives in the report in 3a and write each one down with the thing it describes.

_____
_____
_____

3c Write down two possible reasons for Professor Bell's late arrival.
(If you used Book 2 of *Reading Plus*, you may remember what happened.)

_____
_____

4 Where would you find these in *The Lion*? Write the title of the section under each one.

1 ... from a minuet to a march, a tango to a Norwegian folksong.

_____

2 At eight o'clock, we were up again and eating breakfast, eagerly awaiting our first ski-ing lesson.

_____

3 In their next match, the 2nd X1 showed more skill and determination and were unlucky to lose to a penalty which was given when Jones slipped and accidentally handled the ball.

_____

4 The school is fortunate to have been given a beautiful set of water-colours painted by the late Bernard Donelly, who was Headmaster from 1940 to 1946.

_____

5 Since the arrival of Mr Jessop, the Meteorology Club has become one of the most exciting clubs to join.

_____

6

_____

5a Here are parts of two diaries which were written during the Canal Expedition and printed in *The Lion*. Which one was written by a student and which one by a teacher?

Monday 23rd March

Another wet day! Mr Clarke was furious with us at breakfast because we had got up late, but we got away at 7.00 and it didn't make any difference. The whole morning was spent getting stuck in the low water and then some fool ran us into the bank at the first lock and Caroline and George and I fell overboard. It was not funny! I had to wash everything I had on. It'll never dry in this weather. I'm definitely NOT going to go on any more of Mr Clarke's adventure holidays!

MONDAY 23RD MARCH

A dull, misty morning, but not too cold. We had planned to set off at 6.30 but some of the students were unwilling to get up and we finally left at 7.00. The weather began to improve but we got stuck a number of times because the water was very low. Then, at the very first lock, we had a real problem. As we went close to the bank to let some people go ashore, the boat suddenly stopped dead. The result was that some of the crew who were not paying attention fell overboard. And then the front of the boat got stuck in the mud. It took us over an hour to sort everything out and we had some rather miserable crew members for the rest of the day. Luckily, nobody was hurt and the boat was not damaged at all.

5b Read through the two diary pages again and decide:

1 which one gives the most details about what they did.
   the one on the right

2 which one tells you most about how the writer felt.

3 which one is the most optimistic.

4 which one is critical of other people.

5c At least three sentences in the diary on the left in 5a tell you more about how the writer felt than about what happened. Underline three sentences that are like this.

18

6a Read this poem written by a third form student and printed in *The Lion*.

THINGS I HATE

I hate spiders and I hate snakes.
I hate the chocolate pudding my mother makes.

I hate it when I get a mosquito bite.
I hate students who get everything right.

I hate crowds and I hate rain.
I hate travelling by train.

I hate being lonely, having no friends.
I hate the kind of presents my Grandma sends.

I hate it when a teacher shouts at me.
I hate drinking coffee and I hate drinking tea.

I hate injections and the dentist's chair.
I hate it when someone cuts my hair.

I hate being told to tidy my things.
I hate my Dad listening when my friend rings.

I hate writing poetry and making things rhyme.
I hate, I hate it, I hate it.

6b Answer these questions about the poem.

1. How many times does the writer use the word 'hate'? _____
2. Why does she use 'hate' so many times? _____
3. How many different things does she say she hates? _____

6c Tick (✓) the things in the poem that you hate too.

6d Write down three other things which you hate.

Write one or two verses, like the ones in 'Things I hate', about things you like. If you can, make the lines rhyme.

Agatha Christie's greatest mystery

£100 REWARD

A new photograph of Mrs. Christie.

The "Daily News" offers £100 reward to the first person furnishing us with first information leading to the discovery of the whereabouts, if alive, of Mrs. Christie.

Information should be telephoned to the "Daily News" (Telephone: Central 5000, or telegraphed or conveyed by a personal call at the "Daily News" Office 19, Bouverie Street, E.C.4.)

HOW TO RECOGNISE HER
Age 35
Height 5ft 7ins
Figure .... Well-built
Hair .. Reddish and shingled
Eyes .... Grey
Complexion .... Fair

WEARING:
Green jumper
Green velour hat
Platinum ring with one pearl
Probably carrying a black handbag.

Agatha Christie, the world's most famous writer of detective stories, died in 1976 without ever revealing the true story of her own mysterious disappearance 50 years earlier.

Journalists and biographers have tried, in vain, to establish what exactly happened to Agatha Christie during the eleven days in December 1926 when she went missing.

1a When it became known that Agatha Christie had disappeared, all the newspapers reported the story and joined in the hunt to find her.

Read the details printed in the *Daily News* on 7 December 1926 which offered a £100 reward for any information which would help them locate Mrs Christie.

1b How were readers to contact the newspaper if they had any information?

_____
_____
_____

1c Complete this paragraph about Agatha Christie's appearance.

She is a [1]_____ woman about [2]_____ tall, with [3]_____ ,shingled [4]_____ , [5]_____ eyes and a [6]_____ complexion. She is [7]_____ years old.

1d Now write the rest of this paragraph about what she was wearing.

At the time of her disappearance, she _____
_____
_____
_____

2   Read this short article, which the *Daily News* printed on the same day.

1 Put a line under the things which had been found.
2 Put a circle round the number of men who were going to take part in the search
3 Put a circle round the place where a car had been abandoned.
4 Underline the reason given for posting a police guard outside the family home.

SHOE AND SCARF
FOUND ON DOWNS YESTERDAY.

A woman's patent shoe.
A woman's scarf.

These articles, found by searchers for Mrs. Agatha Christie, the missing novelist, on the Downs near Guildford yesterday, have led the police to organise an intensified search, in which 500 men will take part to-day.

The shoe resembles those Mrs. Christie is believed to have been wearing. It was found about 50 yards down the hillside from Newlands Corner, where the novelist's car was abandoned.

A police guard has been posted outside The Styles, the home of Colonel and Mrs. Christie – at the Colonel's request, he states.

A full report of yesterday's developments appears on Page Five.

3a Here is an article from another newspaper. Before reading the article, take a quick look at the four headlines and write down the two main points that are made.

_____

_____

PUBLIC HUNT FOR MRS. CHRISTIE.

10,000 Motorists to Scour Surrey Downs.
POLICE VIEW.
"Convinced the Missing Novelist is Dead."

To-day the general public are joining in the hunt for the missing woman writer of mystery stories, Mrs. Agatha Christie.

Mrs. CHRISTIE disappeared from her home, The Styles, Sunningdale, Berkshire, on the night of last Friday week. Later her abandoned motor-car was discovered in the road near Newlands Corner, a celebrated Surrey beauty spot in the Guildford district.

Police searches have been carried on incessantly ever since. The Downs have been exhaustively explored, ponds have been dragged, and woods combed and recombed in the hope of finding the missing woman. But all to no avail.

3b There are five different words in the article in 3a which could be replaced by the words 'search' or 'searched'. List these words.

_____   _____   _____

_____   _____

21

In spite of massive searches, no-one could find Agatha Christie, alive or dead. The police stated that they believed that she had crashed her car, stumbled away from it in a daze and lost her way in the woods.

4a Meanwhile, lots of people began to say that they had seen the missing woman. Read what these witnesses said and complete the policeman's notes on the opposite page.

Reported sightings of missing person(s)

<u>Christie, Agatha</u>

Mrs. Kitchener reported that a person fitting the description stopped in front of her and then walked away.

Mr. Fredrick Dove saw an empty car. Then he noticed a young girl nearby. She told him that [1]_____

Hotel manageress reported that [2]_____

Mr. B. Brown reported that about [3]_____ he had offered a young woman a lift but she had [4]_____

Cow-man from local farm saw [5]_____

Mr. Richards reported seeing a young woman with a man in a car [6]_____ on Saturday afternoon. The man was [7]_____

4b Could all the witnesses have been right? Had they all seen Agatha Christie?

Write down any evidence you have for your answers.

_____

_____

_____

Eventually, eleven days after Agatha Christie's disappearance, she was recognised in a hotel in Harrogate, in Yorkshire, where she had registered using the same name as the woman her husband was in love with. Nobody has ever discovered why she went there or how she got there. It remains the greatest mystery of her life.

23

5a Read what Gillian Gill, one of Agatha Christie's biographers wrote, in *Agatha Christie — The Woman and Her Mysteries*, about the disappearance.

> When considering the case of the disappearing detective novelist, it turns out to be useful to learn the lessons Christie herself has taught us in her detective fiction and set down a list of questions and puzzling facts, just as Hercule Poirot might do. Why did Christie drive away from her home in Sunningdale late at night? What did she do in the next five or six hours? Why did she abandon her car and other possessions by the road at Newlands Corner, just beyond Guildford in Surrey, at most an hour's drive from her home? Is there some significance to the fact that Newlands Corner, where Agatha ditched her car, is only a few miles from Godalming, where Agatha's husband and Miss Nancy Neele were staying for the weekend with friends? Having abandoned her rather randomly packed travelling case and coat in the car, how did she manage to make the journey to London and then to Harrogate? How did she afford a new wardrobe and a room in an expensive hotel?

5b Write down the parts of the text which tell you:

1. that Agatha Christie used lists of questions and puzzling facts in her Hercule Poirot stories.

2. where Agatha Christie set off from that night.

3. how far away from home she was when she abandoned her car.

4. that her husband was perhaps having an affair with Nancy Neele.

5. that she had planned to stay away from home at least overnight.

6. that she went to Harrogate via London.

5c   Do you learn anything new about what happened from Gillian Gill's words in 5a?

_____

If so, what?

_____

_____

6   Read this sentence from Agatha Christie's own autobiography. It is the only sentence in her book which MIGHT refer to her disappearance. There is no other reference in any of her writing to what happened at that time.

Do you think the sentence DOES refer to her mysterious disappearance?

> There are things one does not want to go over in one's mind again. Things that you have to accept because they have happened, but you don't want to think of them again.

from Agatha Christie: An Autobiography

Would you be a good witness?

Look at somebody you don't know – in the street, on the bus, in a shop – and then, next day, try to describe the person and what they were wearing in detail.

It's more fun if you ask a friend to look at the same person at the same time so that you can compare your descriptions.

5 Interesting numbers

Can you write the numbers one to ten in any other way?

1 Read and find out how some of the ancient races counted. Use the information to complete the numbers one to ten in each system.

The ancient Egyptian system

The ancient Egyptians used a system of short vertical lines, which each represented one finger. For each number, the lines were put in a group, side by side. This rule was used for all the numbers from one to nine. The number ten was written as a half circle which looked like a small bridge.

| ||

The Babylonian system

More than five thousand years ago, the Babylonians used to print numbers in soft ground using a stick with a 'v' shape on the end of it. Each 'v' counted as one and for numbers of three or more they printed the 'v's in a group, rather than in a straight line. For the number ten, a single shape was printed on its side.

V v v

The ancient Greek system

The ancient Greeks used their alphabet to represent numbers. It's very difficult to do sums using their system! The number one looked like a capital 'A' and two was a capital 'B'. Three was like a capital 'F' without the small line in the middle. Four was a triangle with equal sides. Five was a capital 'E'. Six was a capital 'F' and seven a capital 'Z'. Eight was 'H'. Nine was a circle with a horizontal line across the middle which didn't quite touch the sides. And ten was just like the number one – a straight vertical line.

A

The Mayan system

The Mayans, who lived in Mexico long ago, had a system based on dots and dashes. A dot meant one, two dots two, etc. and they simply put the dots in a horizontal line. A dash meant five and a dash with a dot after it meant six. They had a funny shape like a circle with two marks inside it (rather like a button with two holes) to represent zero. They only used this mark in numbers of twenty and over, so ten was just two dashes side by side. The Mayans used numbers up to twenty much more than the other ancient civilisations did.

•   —

The ancient Roman system

The ancient Romans had a system based on the fingers of just one hand. They counted in groups of five, using vertical lines and 'V's and 'X's. For one, they used a single line and for the numbers two and three they simply used two and three lines. They treated four as 'one before five' and used a vertical line in front of a 'V'. Six was made by putting a single line after the 'V' and seven and eight followed the same rule. Nine was treated as 'one before ten' and so had a single line in front of an 'X'.

I   V

2a Read this explanation about why people counted in different ways.

1 The system of counting which the ancient Egyptians used and which most of us still use is based on the number of fingers we have. People used to use their fingers – and thumbs – to calculate numbers. Some people still do it like that – especially if they haven't got their calculators handy!

2 It is sometimes said that the ancient Romans counted on the fingers of just one hand because they needed to keep their other hand free to grab their swords. Another explanation is that you need the fingers of one hand to touch the fingers of the other hand as you count!

3 The best explanation for why the Mayans counted in sets of twenty is that they didn't wear shoes!

2b What does the explanation in 2a tell us about how each of the following counted?

1 the ancient Romans _____

2 the ancient Egyptians _____

3 the Mayans _____

2c Which paragraph in the text in 2a mentions:

1 swords? _____   3 calculators? _____

2 shoes? _____   4 thumbs? _____

3 Lots of interesting things can be done using the numbers in the Arabic system.

Before trying the example in 4 on the next page, check that you know the meaning of these words. They are all used in mathematics. If you need to, look up the words in your dictionary. Make notes of what they mean or put a symbol to show you understand.

1 digit   *a single number*   7 column _____

2 add _____   8 sequence _____

3 subtract _____   9 pattern _____

4 multiply _____   10 a table _____

5 divide _____   11 the square of a number _____

6 reverse _____

4 Try this. Going through the example may help you follow the instructions.

> Write down any number consisting of three different digits. You are allowed to use zero, even as the first digit, if you wish. Now reverse the order of the number and subtract the smaller of your two numbers from the larger. Reverse the digits of that number and add it to your previous answer. The result will be 1089. Always.
>
> Example:
>
> Suppose you start with the number 746. Reversing it gives 647.
> Now subtract the smaller number (647) from the larger (746). The answer to this is 099. Note that you must keep the zero at the beginning of the number to be sure you always have a three-digit number. Now reverse this number, which gives you 990. And finally add 099 to 990. The answer will be 1089.
>
> _____
> _____
> _____
> _____
> _____

5a Another interesting thing about mathematics is that you can make 'patterns' with numbers.

Try this. (It's much easier to do with a calculator than using your fingers!)

> Multiply 7 by 7 and write down the answer on the first line of the table below.
> Now multiply 67 by 67 and write the answer below the first answer. Now multiply 667 by 667 and add the answer to your table.
> And next multiply 6667 by 6667 and add that answer too.
> Go on as many times as you can, depending on the limits of your calculator.
>
> _____
> _____
> _____
> _____
> _____
>
> Look at the table you have produced. Interesting, isn't it?
>
> You can make the same kind of table using the squares of the numbers 34, 334, 3334, etc.
>
> And, if you are interested, you can also try the same thing with the squares of the numbers 9, 99, 999, 9999, etc.?

5b Now here's something slightly different.

> Make a table of the results of multiplying 15873 by 7, then by 14, then by 21, and 28, and so on (i.e. multiples of 7).
>
> What is interesting about this table?
>
> _____
> _____
> _____
> _____
> _____

6a Look at this table and enjoy it.

Table

1	×	1	=	1
11	×	11	=	121
111	×	111	=	12321
1111	×	1111	=	1234321
11111	×	11111	=	123454321
111111	×	111111	=	12345654321
1111111	×	1111111	=	1234567654321
11111111	×	11111111	=	123456787654321
111111111	×	111111111	=	12345678987654321

6b Complete these instructions which would help someone produce the table in 6a.

Multiply 1 [1]_____ 1 and write down the answer so that it looks like this:

      1   ×   1   =   1

It's important to leave lots of space because the table will get wider as you go on.

Now, [2]_____ 11 by [3]_____ and write that line under the [4]_____ line in your table.

Next, [5]_____ 111 [6]_____ 111 and put it in the [7]_____ .

The next [8]_____ in the [9]_____ must be [10]_____ multiplied by [11]_____ .

Continue in the [12]_____ way until you have [13]_____

111111111 × 111111111.

Doesn't it make a fabulous pattern?

Put this number into your calculator: 5537.
Turn the calculator round through 180°.
What word do you see? _____

Now try these numbers:

918   _____   57738   _____

7735   _____   35007   _____

3705   _____   379919   _____

7108   _____

Can you make any other English words?

6 A part-time job

Have you ever had a part-time job? Baby-sitting? Walking a dog? Helping in a shop? There are quite a lot of jobs that can be done by part-timers.

1a Look through these advertisements and tick (✓) the jobs which could DEFINITELY be done by a student from your school if they were all in your town.

SITUATIONS VACANT

PART-TIME office work.

photocopying, filing, etc.

Excellent English essential.
12 hrs a week, days and times by arrangement.

Write to:
Hall and Hall,
Solicitors, Hill St,
BEEMOUTH.

The Pizza Palace

part-timers wanted to cook and serve.

Free Food

Well paid work.

tel: 348-3197

SITUATIONS VACANT

car cleaners for car showrooms p/t work, hours by arrangement. Tel: 267-9876

coffee bar waiter/ waitress needed NOW. Tues – Sat, 11.30 am-3.00 pm. Some experience preferred. 545-7692 or call in at Cathie's Coffee Bar, High Street, Beemouth.

cleaner to look after large house. Mornings/afternoons. £6 ph + fares. Min 4 hrs per wk. Phone 407-8054

hairdressing assistants required. f/t or p/t. Training given to suitable applicants with good educational background. Apply in writing to:
B Harris,
Betty's Hairdressing Salon,
12, High Street,
Beemouth

shelf stackers wanted at Henley's Supermarket, 5-8 pm, Thurs and Sat. Must be willing to work every week throughout the year. For an interview, call in and ask for the Personnel Manager.

library assistants p/t Sats Would suit school student with an interest in a career in library work. Must be reliable and good with people. Please apply in writing to:
The Librarian,
Beemouth Library,
Station Road, Beemouth.

p/t telephonist/receptionist. Must have cheerful personality and good speaking voice. Hours: 2-6 pm. No week-end work. Please phone:
Right Employment Agency,
621-3375

...orary Work
0 per hour

CAR PARK ATTENDANTS

Must be willing to work unsocial hours.
Excellent pay
Full-time/part-time
Call 348-4627

Par
Exc

1b Which other jobs on the list might it be possible for students from your school to apply for if they had more information? What extra information would they need?

_____
_____
_____
_____
_____

1c Give a reason why each of the remaining jobs could NOT be done by a student from your school.

_____
_____
_____
_____

1d Where would you be working if someone said each of these things to you?

1 'Why don't you brush up all the hair from around the chairs instead of just cleaning the wash-basins all the time?'
   _____

2 'I didn't ask you to clean the inside of the fridge, did I?'
   _____

3 'If you moved the soup along a bit, you could put some of those tins of fruit on that shelf too.'
   _____

4 'You mustn't use that stuff on the windscreen.'
   _____

5 'You needn't do that. The readers put the books back themselves.'
   _____

6 'You are going to photocopy those letters this afternoon, aren't you?'
   _____

7 'I would have helped you to clear those tables if you'd asked.'
   _____

8 'Before you came, we used to do all the photocopying ourselves.'
   _____

1e What is meant by each of the following abbreviations in the job advertisements in 1a?

1 p/t _____   4 min 4 hrs _____
2 f/t _____   5 per wk   _____
3 ph   _____   6 Sats   _____

1f Write down three different ways used in the job advertisements in 1a to say how to apply for the job.

_____
_____
_____

2a Read this letter of application which was received by Hall and Hall.
Do you think they will give this person the job? _____
What are the reasons for your answer?

_____
_____

> 22a, Coronation Road
> Beemouth
> 17, May.
>
> Dear Sir,
> I want a job and I saw your advertisment in the paper. Working in a sollicitor's office would be nice, I think. I used to work in a supermarket, but I hated putting things on the shelfs all the time. My father says doing photocoppying would be easier.
> I could work after school, but not on Fridays. I might be able to work on Sat. mornings sometimes, but I preffer not to.
> I am 16 years old and we have got a photocoppier at school wich I use, so I know how to do it. I can soon teach myself filing.
> I would like to know how much you would pay and when I could start.
> Yours faithfully,
> Philip Lodge.

2b Now correct all the spelling mistakes in Philip Lodge's letter.

3a Here are parts of three other letters which Hall and Hall received from applicants. Which person seems most suitable for the job? _____

Applicant A

I have worked in an office before. I had a summer job in an accountant's office where I was responsible for keeping all the papers in order and producing all the photocopies which were needed as well as inputting data into the computer. Although I wasn't responsible for the filing, I often helped the filing clerk and now understand the principles of filing. If the hours could be arranged so that I didn't start work before 3 pm, I would be happy to accept any arrangement, and even to vary my times of work, to suit you.

Applicant B

When I leave school, I am going to do a secretarial course, so I would like to get some experience of working in an office. I enjoy organising things and have used a word-processor for the last two years. At present, I am the editor of the school magazine, but I'm going to give that up very soon as I want to get a part-time job instead of using all my free time on the magazine. I would like to ask you whether I could complete the 12 hours of work between Monday and Thursday as I wouldn't be able to work on Fridays.

Applicant C

Working in a solicitor's office would be just the job for me because I am going to go to university and study law when I leave school. Even though I would only be doing routine jobs in your office, I might learn something about legal matters. I have done (unpaid) work helping in my father's office, so I know about photocopying and filing and so on.
I play in the school orchestra and there is an overseas tour planned for the first half of July. If I was offered the job in your office, I would need to take two weeks off for the tour. I hope this would be acceptable to you.

3b Each of the applicants in 3a would only accept the job on certain conditions. What are these conditions?

Applicant A _____

_____

Applicant B _____

_____

Applicant C _____

_____

3c Underline the incorrect part of each sentence and then write a sentence giving the correct information.

1 Applicant A had a summer job in a solicitor's office.
_____

2 Applicant B is the editor of a newspaper.
_____

3 Applicant C is going to study medicine when he/she leaves school.
_____

4 Applicant B hates organising things.
_____

5 Applicant A was responsible for the filing in his/her previous job.
_____

3d Which ONE word can you use to fill the gaps in ALL these sentences?

1 Applicant A has had experience of filing _____ Applicant B probably hasn't.

2 Applicant C plays in an orchestra _____ Applicant A probably doesn't.

3 Applicant B is the editor of a school magazine _____ Applicant C probably isn't.

4 Applicant B wouldn't be able to work on Fridays _____ Applicant A would.

4a If you get a part-time job, there are often rules and regulations which you must obey.
Where would you be working if these 'Rules and Regulations' were pinned on the noticeboard?

_____

> **Dress and Appearance Rules for staff on duty**
>
> 1 All staff must wear their white coats at all times.
> 2 Staff must not wear their hair loose. Both men and women with long hair must tie it back tidily.
> 3 Staff handling uncovered food must wear the hats provided. (Other staff needn't wear the hats.)
> 4 Staff may not wear their own cardigans, coats, etc. over their white coats.
> 5 Staff must wear suitable footwear (NOT heavy boots, high heels, etc.)
> 6 Staff must ensure that their hands (and nails) are spotlessly clean.
> 7 Staff must not wear expensive jewellery.

4b Using the 'Rules and Regulations' in 4a as a model, write one rule for people working:

1 as cleaners in an office

_____
_____

2 as waiters or waitresses in a coffee-bar

_____
_____

3 as hairdressing assistants

_____
_____

Write an advertisement for the ideal part-time job for you.

Do you think you can find this job?

7 Frankenstein's monster

If you read these paragraphs from the back cover of a book, would you want to read the book?

1 Look again at the paragraphs on the cover and write down three adjectives which tell you something about the monster.

_____

_____

_____

Many people think that Frankenstein was a monster, but that isn't true. Frankenstein was the man who created a monster in a famous story which is told in a book entitled *Frankenstein*. The book was written in 1816 by Mary Shelley, when she was only nineteen years old.

FRANKENSTEIN

Victor Frankenstein thinks he has found the secret of life. He takes parts from dead people and builds a new 'man'. But this monster is so big and frightening that everyone runs away from him – even Frankenstein himself! The monster is like an enormous baby who needs love. But nobody gives him love, and soon he learns to hate. And, because he is so strong, the next thing he learns is how to kill …

2a Read this account of how Frankenstein got involved in creating a monster. It is a summary of the first part of Mary Shelley's book.

Victor Frankenstein was born in Geneva at the end of the eighteenth century. His father was a rich and successful businessman who married late in life. Victor grew up in a happy and loving family. At school, he became friendly with a fellow student called Henri Clerval and this friendship continued for many years. Both boys were clever and worked hard at their studies. Victor developed a particular interest in sciences, and was especially fascinated by electricity and the question of the source of life.
When Victor left school and went to the University of Ingoldstadt, he continued with these studies and gradually formed a desire to 'unfold the deepest mysteries of creation' and to create a living thing himself. Having spent some time studying dead bodies, he decided that he would try to make a human body and bring it to life. He gathered together the parts he needed to make a 2.4 metre tall 'superhuman' and worked day and night until it was completed.

2b Which words in the text in 2a could be replaced by the words and phrases in the box? For each one, underline the appropriate word in the text and write the synonym in the margin opposite it.

| made up his mind | the origin | collected | reveal | the biggest secrets |
| interested in | little by little | special | | |

2c What kind of creature did Frankenstein want to make?

_____

3a After months of work, Frankenstein was ready to bring his creature to life.
Read Mary Shelley's account of the moment when it breathed for the first time.
(Because the story was written nearly 200 years ago, it includes words and expressions which modern writers would probably not use. The notes on the right will help you to follow the story.)

It was on a dreary night of November, that I beheld (1) the accomplishment of my toils (2). With an anxiety that almost amounted to agony, I collected the instruments of life around me, that I might infuse a spark of being (3) into the lifeless thing that lay at my feet. It was already one in the morning; the rain pattered dismally against the panes, and my candle was nearly burnt out, when, by the glimmer of the half-extinguished light, I saw the dull yellow eye of the creature open; it breathed hard, and a convulsive motion agitated its limbs (4).
How can I describe my emotions at this catastrophe, or how delineate the wretch (5) whom with such infinite pains and care I had endeavoured to form (6)? His limbs were in proportion, and I had selected his features as beautiful. Beautiful! – Great God! His yellow skin scarcely (7) covered the work of muscles and arteries beneath; his hair was of a lustrous black, and flowing; his teeth of a pearly whiteness; but these luxuriances (8) only formed a more horrid contrast with his watery eyes, that seemed almost of the same colour as the dun white (9) sockets in which they were set, his shrivelled complexion and straight black lips.
The different accidents of life are not so changeable as the feelings of human nature. I had worked hard for nearly two years, for the sole purpose of infusing life into an inanimate body. For this I had deprived myself of rest and health. I had desired it with an ardour that far exceeded moderation (10); but now that I had finished, the beauty of the dream vanished, and breathless horror and disgust filled my heart. Unable to endure the aspect of the being (11) I had created, I rushed out of the room.

(1) saw
(2) result of my work
(3) put the beginning of life
(4) a violent movement shook its arms and legs
(5) describe the awful being
(6) tried to make
(7) hardly
(8) rich features
(9) yellowish
(10) wanted it far too much
(11) not able to look at the man

3b Read this simplified version of the section of the story in 3a.
Underline the parts in Mary Shelley's original version which are told again, in simpler language, in this text.

At first nothing happened. But after a few minutes I saw the creature's body begin to move. Slowly, terribly, the body came alive. Its arms and legs began to move, and slowly it sat up.
The dead body had been an ugly thing, but alive, it was much more horrible. Suddenly I wanted to escape from it. I ran out of the laboratory, and locked the door. I was filled with fear at what I had done.

3c Find the following snippets of Mary Shelley's text in 2a and answer the questions.

1 '... pattered against the panes ...'. What pattered against the panes? _____

2 ' ... it breathed hard ...'. What breathed hard? _____

3 '... in which they were set ...'. In which what were set? _____

4 'For this I had deprived myself of rest and health.' For what? _____

5 'I had desired it ...'. Desired what? _____

When Frankenstein went back into his laboratory the next day, the monster had disappeared. Frankenstein was very glad that he had gone and he tried to forget about the whole disaster.

4a Some time later, a terrible tragedy occurred. Read about what happened to Frankenstein's brother.

> Some time later, Frankenstein received a letter from his father telling him that his young brother, William, had been murdered. All the family was shocked when Justine Moritz, the boy's nanny, was accused of the crime and Frankenstein was horrified when she was executed for the murder because he felt that his monster had done it, not Justine. Throughout the following months, Frankenstein became more and more depressed.
>
> Then, one day when he was travelling in the mountains, trying to forget his troubles, Frankenstein suddenly met the monster. He shouted furiously at him, accusing him of the crime, and telling him to stay away from him and his family. But the monster insisted on talking to his creator and told him the sad story of his life since he had run away from the laboratory where Frankenstein had made him.
>
> The monster said that he had tried, in vain, to attach himself to humans, but nobody would have anything to do with him, because they found him so ugly and frightening. He told Frankenstein that even when he had saved a child who was drowning in a river, nobody thanked him. In fact, the father shot him in the shoulder because he was afraid of him.
>
> The monster became more and more lonely and more and more unhappy. Then, by chance, he came across William playing in a field and he decided to capture the boy and try to make him become his friend. He took hold of William and tried to embrace him, but the boy screamed and, in an attempt to silence him, the monster held him by the throat and, accidentally, strangled him.

4b Look carefully at the first paragraph of the text in 4a and answer these questions:

1 Who was accused of murdering William?
    _____

2 Who did Frankenstein think had done it?
    _____

3 How did Frankenstein feel about this?
    _____

4c Look carefully at the last two paragraphs of the text in 4a and write down:

1 why the monster was unhappy. _____

2 why he felt particularly upset when a man shot him through the shoulder.

_____

3 what he wanted to do when he met William. _____

4 how he, accidentally, strangled William. _____

4d Look again at the text in 4a and:

put **1** beside the part which says what finally happened to Justine
put **2** beside the part which says where Frankenstein met the monster after the murder
part **3** beside the part which explains how the monster had been shot in the shoulder
put **4** beside the part which tells how the monster killed William

5a The monster told Frankenstein how lonely he was and asked Frankenstein to make a mate for him. Read what happened next.

The monster told Frankenstein that, if he would make a mate for him, he would go to the jungles of South America and would have nothing more to do with other people.
Frankenstein agreed to this request and went off to Scotland to work on the new creature. His friend, Henri Clerval, travelled with him but knew nothing about what Frankenstein was doing.
Frankenstein became more and more terrified. Perhaps this new creature would be even worse than the first one. Perhaps she wouldn't agree to go off to the jungle to live. Perhaps she would murder even more people. Soon, Frankenstein realised that he could not complete the task and he destroyed the creature he was making. Just then, the monster appeared and begged him to keep his promise and continue to work on the mate he wanted so much. When Frankenstein refused, the monster said: 'I go; but remember I shall be with you on your wedding night!' and he disappeared.
Frankenstein and Clerval moved on to Ireland, but the monster followed them and killed Clerval. Frankenstein was accused of the murder and spent three months in jail before being proved innocent and being released.
Soon, he returned to Switzerland. Some time later, he married his childhood sweetheart, Elizabeth, but on their wedding night, while Frankenstein was searching the inn to make sure the monster was not there, Elizabeth was strangled in her bed.

5b Put 'Yes' beside the things you can tell for sure from the text in 5a and 'No' beside the ones that you cannot be sure about. For each 'Yes', write down the part of the text which gives you the information.

1 where the monster would go if he had a mate to go with him _____ _____

2 whether Clerval knew what Frankenstein was making _____ _____

3 whether the new creature would be a murderer _____ _____

4 How far Frankenstein had got with making the new creature when he decided to destroy her
_____ _____

5 whether Frankenstein actually murdered Clerval _____ _____

6 whether Frankenstein remembered the monster's warning about being with him on his wedding night
_____ _____

6a Read the end of the story.

Frankenstein felt that he must revenge the deaths of his loved ones and so he left his home and set out in search of the monster, determined that he would not rest until one or other of them was dead. Throughout his search, he received constant reminders that the monster knew where he was at every moment but he never caught up with him. Finally, on board a ship trapped by the Arctic ice, Frankenstein died without gaining the revenge he was seeking.
Soon after Frankenstein's death, the monster appeared on the ship to mourn over his creator's corpse. He told the captain of the ship that Frankenstein was the only parent he had ever known and he had only wanted his affection. Now, it was too late. The monster leapt overboard, saying that he was going to kill himself, and he was never seen again.

6b Answer these 'why' questions.

1 Why did Frankenstein take a ship going to the Arctic Circle?
_____

2 Why did the monster mourn over Frankenstein's corpse?
_____

3 Why did the monster leap off the ship to kill himself?
_____

7 Choose a heading from this list for each of the sections of text in 2 to 6 and write it above the appropriate text.

More deaths   **A sad end**   **A life is created**
A scientific experiment **The monster's promise**   **A life without love**
A fatal embrace   **The dreadful truth**   **The monster's revenge**

The Frankenstein Game – you are the monster!

Here's a game to play. You can play alone and try to improve your score or you can play against someone else.

You need a book and something to use as a 'counter' (perhaps a small coin).

Put your counter on 'Start'.

Open your book at page 7, and count how many letters there are in the last word on the page. Move your counter that many places and put a mark on the score box. Follow any instructions you 'land' on.

Do the same thing, using pages: 12, 22, 14, 23, 35, 16, 29, 24, 18, 28, 33, 11, 15, 21, 26, 20, 31, 13, 27, 19, 25

(If a page has no words on it, use the next page.)

SCORE BOX (Put a mark here each time you move your counter.)

☐☐☐☐☐☐☐☐☐☐☐☐☐☐☐☐☐☐☐☐☐☐☐☐☐
     5   10   15   20   25

How many moves did you have to make to complete the game? _____

Try again using another book and see if you can do better.

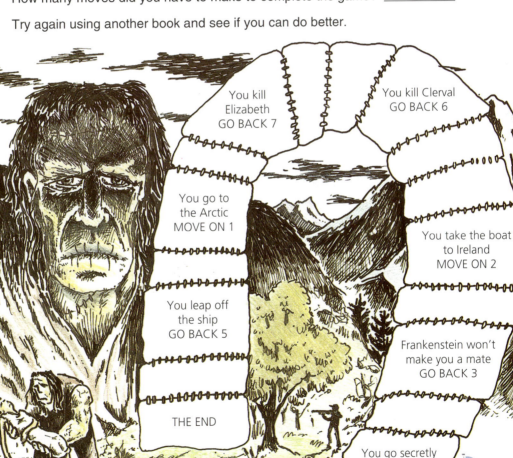

8 Well done!

Exams — ugh! Do you hate doing exams? Would you rather be the teacher who marks the papers?

1a Look at the beginning of this English exam and complete Question 1.

ENGLISH

Question 1 Complete this paragraph by putting in the correct prepositions.

We live _____ a flat _____ the tenth floor. My friend, Jack, lives _____ the eighth floor, two floors _____ us. If I want to see him, I run _____ the stairs because it's not worth getting the lift. Last time I went to see him, his mother was sitting cross-legged _____ the floor, looking _____ the wall. I think she was doing Yoga. The rest _____ the family was sitting _____ the television, eating supper. Nobody spoke to me, so I just sat _____ Jack and waited.

(10 marks)

1b Check your answers with the Answer Key on page 47. Correct any you got wrong.

1c Here are the answers to Question 1 given by Student A, Student B and Student C. Correct the work and give each one a mark out of 10.

Student A

Question 1 Complete this paragraph by putting in the correct prepositions.

We live _in_ a flat _on_ the tenth floor. My friend, Jack, lives _on_ the eighth floor, two floors _above_ us. If I want to see him, I run _up_ the stairs because it's not worth getting the lift. Last time I went to see him, his mother was sitting cross-legged _on_ the floor, looking _to_ the wall. I think she was doing Yoga. The rest _of_ the family was sitting _before_ the television, eating supper. Nobody spoke to me, so I just sat _by_ Jack and waited.

(10 marks)

Student B

Question 1 Complete this paragraph by putting in the correct prepositions.

We live _in_ a flat _on_ the tenth floor. My friend, Jack, lives _on_ the eighth floor, two floors _above_ us. If I want to see him, I run _up_ the stairs because it's not worth getting the lift. Last time I went to see him, his mother was sitting cross-legged _on_ the floor, looking _at_ the wall. I think she was doing Yoga. The rest _of_ the family was sitting _in front of_ the television, eating supper. Nobody spoke to me, so I just sat _by_ Jack and waited.

(10 marks)

Student C

Question 1 Complete this paragraph by putting in the correct prepositions.

We live _in_ a flat _at_ the tenth floor. My friend, Jack, lives _at_ the eighth floor, two floors _over_ us. If I want to see him, I run _up_ the stairs because it's not worth getting the lift. Last time I went to see him, his mother was sitting cross-legged _on_ the floor, looking _to_ the wall. I think she was doing Yoga. The rest _of_ the family was sitting _by_ the television, eating supper. Nobody spoke to me, so I just sat _down_ Jack and waited.

(10 marks)

42

2 Here are the answers for Question 2 from the exam. Use them to correct the three students' papers. This time, you must give a mark out of 20 for each student by allocating 2 marks for each correct answer and deducting a mark if the spelling is wrong.

1	should	5	could	9	would
2	could	6	should	10	should
3	would	7	would		
4	would	8	could		

Student A

Question 2   Put *could*, *should* or *would* in each of these sentences.
1. People say you __should__ always be polite to your parents.
2. I __could__ swim when I was only three years old.
3. I promised I __would__ be here on time, so I will.
4. I __should__ rather tell him myself.
5. __Could__ I have some more potatoes, please?
6. It's going to rain, so I think you __should__ take my umbrella.
7. I asked if they __should__ like me to wait for them.
8. When he went in, he __could__ hear voices in the kitchen.
9. She __would__ love to meet you.
10. I'm afraid we've finished; if you wanted to play, you __sould__ have come earlier.

(20 marks)

Student B

Question 2   Put *could*, *should* or *would* in each of these sentences.
1. People say you __should__ always be polite to your parents.
2. I __could__ swim when I was only three years old.
3. I promised I __would__ be here on time, so I will.
4. I __would__ rather tell him myself.
5. __Could__ I have some more potatoes, please?
6. It's going to rain, so I think you __should__ take my umbrella.
7. I asked if they __would__ like me to wait for them.
8. When he went in, he __could__ hear voices in the kitchen.
9. She __would__ love to meet you.
10. I'm afraid we've finished; if you wanted to play, you __should__ have come earlier.

(20 marks)

Student C

Question 2   Put *could*, *should* or *would* in each of these sentences.
1. People say you __should__ always be polite to your parents.
2. I __could__ swim when I was only three years old.
3. I promised I __could__ be here on time, so I will.
4. I __would__ rather tell him myself.
5. __Should__ I have some more potatoes, please?
6. It's going to rain, so I think you __should__ take my umbrella.
7. I asked if they __would__ like me to wait for them.
8. When he went in, he __could__ hear voices in the kitchen.
9. She __would__ love to meet you.
10. I'm afraid we've finished; if you wanted to play, you __would__ have come earlier.

(20 marks)

43

3a Now for Question 3 on the exam paper. This question is worth 20 marks. Before you begin to check the students' answers, go through the question (which is in 3b below) and decide how you will allocate these marks.

Will you give two marks for each perfectly correct answer? Will you give one mark when the answer is more or less correct? Will you take off marks for spelling mistakes?

Write down your marking scheme now and then use it when you go through the three students' papers.

_____

_____

_____

3b Try to mark Question 3 BEFORE you look at the correct answers (which are in the Answer Key to the exam questions on page 47). Remember to give marks out of 20.

Student A

Question 3 Write questions beginning with 'Why ...' to ask the reason for each of the actions.

e.g. He bought a new coat.
Why did he buy a new coat?

1. They went to France.
Why did thy go to France?

2. She wanted to speak to me.
Why she did want to speak to me?

3. He felt ill.
Why he did feel ill?

4. She should have left earlier.
Why she should have left earlier?

5. They began to laugh.
Why thy did begin to lagh?

6. She forgot to post the letter.
Why did she forget to post the letter?

7. He chose a computer.
Why did he chose a computer?

8. They stood under a tree.
Why did thy stand under a tree?

9. They thought I had gone home.
Why did they think I had gone home?

10. We slept in a field.
Why did you sleep in a field?

(20 marks)

44

Student B

Question 3 Write questions beginning with 'Why ...' to ask the reason for each of the actions.

e.g. He bought a new coat.

<u>Why did he buy a new coat?</u>

1 They went to France.
<u>Why did they go to France?</u>

2 She wanted to speak to me.
<u>Why did she want to speak to you?</u>

3 He felt ill.
<u>Why did he felt ill?</u>

4 She should have left earlier.
<u>Why did she have left earlier?</u>

5 They began to laugh.
<u>Why did they begin to laugh?</u>

6 She forgot to post the letter.
<u>Why did she forget to post the letter?</u>

7 He chose a computer.
<u>Why did he chosen a computer?</u>

8 They stood under a tree.
<u>Why they stood under a tree?</u>

9 They thought I had gone home.
<u>Why did they think you had gone home?</u>

10 We slept in a field.
<u>Why did we sleep in a field?</u>

(20 marks)

Student C

Question 3 Write questions beginning with 'Why ...' to ask the reason for each of the actions.

e.g. He bought a new coat.
Why did he buy a new coat?

1 They went to France.
   Why did they go to France?

2 She wanted to speak to me.
   Why did she want to speak to you?

3 He felt ill.
   Why did he feel ill?

4 She should have left earlier.
   Why should she have left earlier?

5 They began to laugh.
   Why did they begin to laugh?

6 She forgot to post the letter.
   Why did she forget to post the letter?

7 He chose a computer.
   Why did he chose a computer?

8 They stood under a tree.
   Why did they stand under a tree?

9 They thought I had gone home.
   Why did they think you had gone home?

10 We slept in a field.
    Why did you sleep in a field?

(20 marks)

4 The total marks for the three questions is 50. Add up the students' marks and double them to give a percentage for each one.

Results	ENGLISH
Student A	_____
Student B	_____
Student C	_____

5a Here are some remarks which the teacher might put at the end of an exam paper. For each of the students, choose two remarks which would be suitable (one from Box 1 and one from Box 2) and write them below.

BOX 1
Rather disappointing
A good effort!
A lovely surprise!
Well done!
Not a good result

BOX 2
You really must finish in the time allowed. You lost about 20% by not completing the paper.

Your answers to Q1 and Q2 are excellent. You should revise the irregular verbs again.

You have obviously learnt the irregular verbs. You should now concentrate on practising prepositions.

Please see me to get extra work for the school holiday.

Your exam result is much better than your term's work. Be careful with spellings – particularly 'they', and with word order in questions.

For Student A _____

For Student B _____

For Student C _____

Write a question for the next exam. It must test students' knowledge of how plurals of nouns are formed.

Decide how many marks your question should receive in total and what the marking scheme should be.

Ask a couple of friends to try your question, separately. How many marks do they each get? Do they think it was a fair question?

Answer key to the exam questions

1a Question 1

We live in a flat on the tenth floor. My friend, Jack, lives on the eighth floor, two floors below us. If I want to see him, I run down the stairs because it's not worth getting the lift. Last time I went to see him, his mother was sitting cross-legged on the floor, looking at/towards the wall. I think she was doing Yoga. The rest of the family was sitting in front of/round the television, eating supper. Nobody spoke to me, so I just sat by /beside Jack and waited.

Question 3

1 Why did they go to France?
2 Why did she want to speak to you?
3 Why did he feel ill?
4 Why should she have left earlier?
5 Why did they begin to laugh?
6 Why did she forget to post the letter?
7 Why did he choose a computer?
8 Why did they stand under a tree?
9 Why did they think you had gone home?
10 Why did you/we sleep in a field?

9 Staying at the Wessex

The Wessex Hotel is a medium-size hotel in Beemouth, a small sea-side town in England.

1a Read this story about three people who were charged the wrong price at the Wessex. As you read, write very brief answers to the questions on the left.

1 Who had the three friends arranged to meet?

_____

2 How many beds were there in the room?

_____

3 Who told them the price?

_____

4 How much had she overcharged them?

_____

5 How much did the hotel employee keep for himself?

_____

Three student friends, Andy, Ben and Edward, were travelling round the coast of England on holiday. They had arranged to meet two other friends, Cathie and Denise, in Beemouth. They arrived in the town very late one evening and discovered that it had just one hotel – The Wessex. They went in and asked for three rooms. Unfortunately, there was only one room available but the receptionist assured them that it was a large room with three beds and so they decided to take it.

'That'll be just £30,' the receptionist told them. 'We have a special offer on at present.' Andy, Ben and Edward were delighted with the price. They decided to pay immediately and they each gave the receptionist £10. Then they went to the room to unpack.

A little later, the receptionist realized that she had made a mistake and had overcharged them by £5. She asked a colleague to return the £5 to the three guests. Sadly, this colleague was not a very honest person. He realized that the guests were unlikely to be concerned about the amount they had paid because the price was so low, so he decided to give them back £1 each and to keep £2 for himself.

All this meant that Andy, Ben and Edward eventually paid £9 each, which totalled £27 for the room. If you add the £2 which the hotel employee kept, the total is only £29.

1b What happened to the missing pound? Who had it? Where did it go? (If you can't work it out, turn to page 53 where you will find the answer.)

48

1c Find suitable places to add the following words to the story and write each one in the text in 1a. E.g. 'their suitcases' can be put after 'to unpack' at the end of the second paragraph.

   1 their suitcases
   2 single
   3 dishonest
   4 for the room, with bathroom
   5 new, young
   6 just for one night

1d Next day, Andy, Ben and Edward met Cathie and Denise in the new Wessex Shopping Centre, as they had arranged. Just for fun, they all bought identical T-shirts to wear.

2a A couple of days later, when they were out on the beach wearing their new T-shirts, somebody asked them where they had got them from.

Read what they answered and then put a circle round the correct shop in the Shopping Centre.

Andy:	We got them in the new Shopping Centre, in one of those little shops. I can't remember which one. In fact, I think almost all of them sold T-shirts! The only thing I can remember about the shop is that it had lights all round the window and lots of white sun-hats with spots on them.
Cathie:	And there was lots of swimwear in the window too.
Ben:	I know which shop it was. It was the one which sold black shorts. Don't you remember? I was thinking of buying some.
Denise:	There were lots of trainers too. They were awfully expensive!
Edward:	Andy, you're wrong. It didn't have any lights round the window.
Denise:	And the sun-hats were just plain white. The ones with spots on them were in that place by the coffee shop.
Andy:	Yes, you're right, Edward. I made a mistake. The lights were round the window of that shop with the funny salesman. The shop where we got our T-shirts didn't have lights round the window. And, I remember now, the sun-hats were just plain white, like you said, Denise. Sorry!

2b When people are speaking, they often use question tags. Find places in 2a where you can put each of these question tags and write them in.

> weren't they?   wasn't it?   didn't I?   wasn't there?   weren't there?

2c Find these parts of the statements in 2a and answer the questions.

1 '... almost all of them ... .' All of what?

2 '... is that it had lights ... .' What had lights?

3 '... with spots on them ... .' On what?

4 'I was thinking of buying some!' Some what?

5 'They were awfully expensive!' What were awfully expensive?

2d Look through the answers given by the five friends in 2a and underline three sentences which are comments, not factual statements.

3a A few days later, there was another mix-up at the Wessex Hotel. The cashier was ill and the receptionist had to try to sort out the bills for the guests.

At eight o'clock in the morning, two guests came to Reception and asked for their bills. They were both in a terrible hurry. They quickly signed their credit card vouchers, without even looking at their bills.

Read this fax which arrived at the Wessex Hotel later that day and correct the errors on Mr Braun's bill.

11 August

To: The Wessex Hotel, Beemouth

From: Berndt Braun

For the personal attention of the Manager

What on earth has happened to the Wessex lately? I have been a regular guest at your hotel for the past seventeen years but I doubt whether I shall ever stay with you again. When I was at the Wessex in July, all my shirts were ruined by your laundry service (and I have yet to receive compensation). And now, after an overnight stop, I have been charged for a number of things I didn't have!

Your cashier knows that I sometimes have to leave quite early and she always has my bill ready. Today, there was no cashier at the desk and I had to wait a long time while your incompetent receptionist tried to sort out the bills. Eventually, I got my bill and paid it by credit card and then rushed off to keep my first appointment, for which I was already late.

When I got into my office tonight and handed the bill to my secretary, she pointed out that it contained items which were very unusual for me. I now realize that I have paid for a number of things which were put on the bill in error.

Please sort this mess out and cancel my credit card payment. Then send me the proper bill, which I will pay in due course.

For your information, I return my copy of the bill and ask you to note the following points:

I do NOT drink alcohol, so I obviously did not order any wine or brandy.

I arrived at 9 pm and had to have a snack in my room as your restaurant had already closed. I recollect that this snack – a chicken salad – was listed at £6.50.

Because I needed to make an early start, I had to have a continental breakfast (£2.80?) as your chef had not started work.

The Wessex Hotel Beemouth

GUEST: **Mr B. Braun**
ROOM NUMBER: **110**

ROOM:	£30.00
RESTAURANT:	
Afternoon tea	£4.00
Dinner – Table d'hôte	£21.30
Wine (1 bottle)	£9.20
Brandy x1	£3.50
English b'fast	£4.50
ROOM SERVICE:	—
TOTAL:	£72.50

VAT INCLUDED

3b Underline at least five parts of the fax from Mr Braun which show you how angry he is.

3c Look again at the last three paragraphs of Mr Braun's fax. In each one, put a circle round the word which connects the 'action' and the reason for it.

4a Next morning, the Manager received another fax. This one was from Mr Brown. Read the fax and correct his bill.

From: Frederick Brown, Brown Brothers, Gateshead.
Date: 12 August
To: The Manager, Wessex Hotel, Beemouth

I spent the night of 10 August at your hotel and paid my bill (copy sent herewith) the following morning by credit card. I was in a great hurry as I had a train to catch so I didn't check the bill carefully.

As I was sitting in the train, I looked at the bill I had paid and noticed that it contained a number of errors and omissions.

I had tea when I arrived and I also had dinner, with a bottle of wine and a glass of brandy. In the morning, I had a full English breakfast.

I did not use room service at all and, of course, I didn't have a continental breakfast.

Will you please send me a replacement bill and advise me what I owe you.

The Wessex Hotel Beemouth

GUEST: Mr F. Brown
ROOM NUMBER: 101

ROOM: £30.00
RESTAURANT: £2.80
1 Continental b'fast

ROOM SERVICE: £6.50

TOTAL: £39.30
VAT INCLUDED

4c Use information from Mr Brown's fax to complete these sentences.

1 When Mr Brown paid his bill, he didn't _____

2 When he was sitting in the train, he _____

3 When he looked carefully at his bill, he _____
   _____.

4 He wrote in his fax that, when he arrived at the hotel, he _____

5 He also told the Manager that, when he had dinner, he _____
   _____.

6 And when he got up in the morning, he _____

4d What had happened? How had the receptionist made so many mistakes in the two bills?

_____

_____

_____

_____

_____

CHALLENGE!

Write a short fax back to Mr Braun apologizing for the errors and persuading him to continue to use the Wessex Hotel.

Answer to the 'lost £1' puzzle in 1b

Each student paid £10, so the amount they gave the receptionist was £30. Each student was given back £1 and the dishonest person kept £2. This meant that each student had paid £9. So, the cost of the room was £27 MINUS the £2 which the dishonest person had kept for himself – i.e. £25. The mistake which many people make is to ADD £27 and £2 and get the answer £29, when they had expected the answer to be £30.

53

10 Visitors

Who were the last three people to visit your home? Were you pleased to see them?

1a Read this first verse of a poem called 'Coming From Kansas', by Myra Cohn Livingston. Who do you think 'they' refers to?

_____

> Whenever they come from Kansas
> they stay for nearly a week
> and they live with Grandma in Council Bluffs
> because her house has room enough,
> and we go over the day they arrive.
> Everyone shouts when they pull in the drive.
> We kiss and hug and I get to play
> with my cousin Joan most every day
> *and the grown-ups cry when they leave.*

1b Read through the verse again and answer these questions very briefly.

1 What country is it about?

_____

2 Where do the visitors stay?

_____

3 Why do they stay there? _____

4 Why does everyone shout when they pull in the drive? _____

5 Are they happy to see each other? _____

6 How do you know? _____

1c Read the second verse of the poem.

> Whenever they say they're coming,
> we make a lot of plans.
> Joan and I like to put on a play
> and we start to write it the very first day.
> There're costumes and sets of curtains to do;
> we write a part for the neighbor boy, too,
> Denny, who comes in the very first scene
> to introduce Joan, who's always the queen
> *and I have to be the king.*

1d Underline all the words in the verse in 1c which are something to do with putting on a play.

1e Why are the last lines of the first verse and the second verse both printed in italics?

_____

_____

1f Here is another verse (the fourth one) of the poem. Read it and then write a sentence explaining what the two cousins fight about.

_____

_____

> Whenever they come in summer,
> Joan tells me about her friends.
> She says that Kansas is better, too,
> there's always more fun and things to do.
> But when we visited there last year
> I saw her friends, and they all were queer,
> and I told her so, and her face got tight
> and then we had a terrible fight
> and we pulled each other's hair.

54

2a Read this description of a visit made by a schoolgirl to her teacher's home. It comes from Roald Dahl's *Matilda*.

When you have read it all through, write below what the main purpose of each paragraph is.

Miss Honey has just made tea for Matilda and herself.

1   "Let's have it in the sitting-room," Miss Honey said, picking up the tray and leading the way out of the kitchen and down the dark little tunnel into the room at the front. Matilda followed her, but just inside the doorway of the so-called sitting-room she stopped and stared around her in absolute amazement. The room was as small and square and bare as a prison cell. The pale daylight that entered came from a single tiny window in the front wall, but there were no curtains. The only objects in the entire room were two upturned wooden boxes to serve as chairs and a third box between them for a table. That was all. There were no pictures on the walls, no carpet on the floor, only rough unpolished wooden planks, and there were gaps between the planks where dust and bits of grime had gathered. The ceiling was so low that with a jump Matilda could nearly touch it with her finger-tips. The walls were white but the whiteness didn't look like paint. Matilda rubbed her palm against it and a white powder came off on to her skin. It was whitewash, the cheap stuff that is used in cowsheds and stables and hen-houses.

2   Matilda was appalled. Was this really where her neat and trimly-dressed school teacher lived? Was this all she had to come back to after a day's work? It was unbelievable. And what was the reason for it? There was something very strange going on around here, surely.

3   Miss Honey put the tray on one of the upturned boxes. "Sit down, my dear, sit down," she said, "and we'll have a nice hot cup of tea. Help yourself to bread. Both slices are for you. I never eat anything when I get home. I have a good old tuck-in at the school lunch and that keeps me going until the next morning."

4   Matilda perched herself carefully on an upturned box and more out of politeness than anything else she took a slice of bread and margarine and started to eat it. At home she would have been having buttered toast and strawberry jam and probably a piece of sponge-cake to round it off. And yet this was somehow far more fun. There was a mystery here in this house, a great mystery, there was no doubt about that, and Matilda was longing to find out what it was.

Paragraph 1 _____

Paragraph 2 _____

Paragraph 3 _____

Paragraph 4 _____

2b Look carefully at the first paragraph in 2a and underline all the things which Matilda noticed about Miss Honey's sitting-room which surprised her.

2c Look at the second and third paragraphs and find the words Roald Dahl uses to describe:

1 how Matilda felt. _____

2 Miss Honey's appearance. _____

3 the tea. _____

2d Look at the fourth paragraph and write down what Matilda usually had for tea at home.

_____

2e Why did Matilda think that there was 'something strange going on'?

_____

_____

3a Here is a short story about a man who failed to make the visit he wanted to make. When you have read it, think of two ways he could have solved his problem and write them down.

The visit that didn't happen

In March 1984, Dr John Fellows, who lived in England, decided to visit his married daugter in the USA. He bought a return air ticket to New York and flew to Kennedy Airport. When he arrived, however, he realised that he had forgotten his daughter's adress. As he tried to call it to mind, he discovered that he couldn't remember her family name either!

Dr Fellows spent sevral hours at the airport trying to think what his daughter's name was and where it was that she lived, but to no avail. Eventually, he decided that he would have to give up his plan to visit her and he caught the next plain back to England.

The only explanation he could give for his forgetfulness was that he was very tired.

Suggestion 1 _____

_____

Suggestion 2 _____

_____

3b Did you notice the five spelling mistakes in the short story in 3a? Please correct them.

4a Sometimes the things visitors say can be really embarrassing. Has anyone ever said any of these things to you or about you? Tick the ones you have heard before.

4b Think of two more embarrassing things that you hate people to say to you? Add them to the ones in 4a.

5a Read this introduction to a chapter entitled 'How to make sure you are not invited back to the home of boring relatives and friends of your parents'.

Decide what kind of book it is from

For some strange reason parents insist on taking their children to visit relatives and friends of theirs who are among the most boring people the human race has ever produced. What is worse, parents insist during these visits that their children: (a) dress in 'smart' uncomfortable clothes; (b) remain silent during the visit, with only the occasional spot of quiet breathing allowed.

It has always struck us that this is a perfect example of the hypocrisy of parents. They spend years teaching their children to walk and talk, and as soon as they can they tell them: 'Sit down and keep quiet.'

Why do they insist on their children accompanying them on these awful visits? When their child complains, parents say, 'If you don't shut up we'll leave you here and go without you.' When the child says, 'Good, that's what I want,' the parents ignore this remark and force their offspring into hideous clothes, bundle them into the nearest form of transport, and force them to endure mind-numbing boredom for what seems like two eternities.

from The Complete How to Handle Grown-ups by Jim and Duncan Eldridge

5b Complete these sentences with light-hearted ideas about teachers and homework.

1 For some strange reason, teachers insist on students *doing homework* _____ .

2 What is worse, they insist _____ .

3 It has always struck me that _____ .

4 Why do they insist on _____ .

5 When a student complains about having too much homework, the teacher says _____ .

5c Complete these sentences, which are all about the text in 5a.

1 In the first line, 'strange' doesn't mean 'foreign'; it means ...
   _____

2 In the first paragraph, 'smart' is put in inverted commas because ...
   _____

3 In the second paragraph where it says 'and as soon as they can they tell them', the first 'they' refers to _____ and the second one refers to _____ .

4 In the third paragraph, the words 'If you don't shut up we'll leave you here and go without you' are not an offer; they are _____ .

5 In the same paragraph, the word 'offspring' could be replaced by _____ .

6 Again in the third paragraph, the words 'force them to endure mind-numbing boredom' could be re-written as
   _____ .

CHALLENGE!

Think of ten excuses which you could use if you wanted to persuade your parents NOT to make you visit your relatives. Even though you love them all, they can sometimes be rather boring!

11 Nasty moments in sport

We may envy the exciting and glamourous lifestyle of the world's top sportsmen and women but, even for them, things can go horribly wrong.

1a One very unfortunate athlete was Monica Seles, the tennis player. Do you remember what happened to her? If you do, write one sentence describing her horrible experience. If not, come back and write the sentence when you have read the article in 1b.

_____

_____

1b Here is the beginning of the front-page article from *The Times* of Saturday May 1 1993. Read it and complete the sentence in 1a or simply check that you got the facts right.

Spectator stabs tennis star on court

BY EDWARD BUSCALL AND OUR FOREIGN STAFF

MONICA Seles, the top-ranked tennis player, was stabbed in the back by a spectator while playing in a tournament in Hamburg yesterday.

The 19-year-old was sitting in her chair during a change-over when a man lunged at her with a long-bladed knife. She received a 1 inch cut between her shoulders and was taken to a hospital near by after being attended on court.

"She was very lucky," said the tournament doctor, Peter Wind. "Neither the lungs nor the shoulder blades were affected. Monica, who is still suffering from shock, will stay overnight for observation."

1c Put 'Yes' beside the things you can tell for sure from the text in 1b and 'No' beside the ones you can't be sure about.

1 How old Monica Seles was at the time of the attack. _____
2 Whether Monica Seles was the Number 1 player at the time. _____
3 Whether the attack happened at the beginning of a match. _____
4 Whether the attacker was young or old. _____
5 Whether Monica Seles became unconscious as a result of the attack. _____
6 Whether she was rushed to hospital immediately. _____
7 Which parts of her body were affected by the stabbing. _____
8 How long she would have to stay in hospital. _____

1d Read the last part of the report and put a tick (✓) beside any of the things on the list in 1c which, as a result of reading this part, you NOW know for sure.

Later reports suggested that her attacker, an eastern German, was a fan of her German tennis rival, Steffi Graf, and had wanted to stop Seles from playing.
The 38-year-old attacker leaned over a 3ft barrier and stabbed her as she took a break. She screamed and ran to mid-court, reaching for her upper back. She appeared woozy as she stood at courtside and then collapsed. Her brother Zoltan and officials rushed to her, giving her first aid and taking her from the court on a stretcher.
"We saw a man come from the left," said a woman sitting in the front row of the tournament. "He looked strange or drunk. He just looked weird. Then we saw him strike out at Monica."
The attacker was pounced on by security men and members of the crowd, and carried away by four guards.

1e What part did each of the following people play in the incident? Use the texts in 1b and 1d to find the answers.

1 Peter Wind
2 Zoltan, Monica Seles's brother
3 the woman in the front row
4 the security men
5 members of the crowd
6 the four guards

2a Another nasty incident occurred in January 1994, not long before the Winter Olympics in Norway.
Look at this headline and the photos and write down who the victim was and what you think happened to her.

THE DAILY TELEGRAPH   SATURDAY, JANUARY 8, 1994

NEWS

Olympic ice star is attacked by stalker at rink

By Hugh Davies in New York.

61

2b Here are the opening paragraphs of the article about the incident. Read it and re-write the first paragraph in very simple English.

_____
_____
_____

> AN UNPROVOKED attack by a man wielding a club has forced America's leading figure skater to pull out of the trial event for the Winter Olympics.
>
> Nancy Kerrigan, 24, was hit on her right knee just after leaving the ice at Cobo Hall, Detroit, where she was practising on the eve of the US Figure Skating championships. She fell to the floor screaming: "God, why me? Why me?"
>
> The 1992 Olympic bronze medallist, America's top figure skating hope for a gold medal at Lillehammer, Norway, next month, had stopped to talk to a reporter when a tall, white man wearing a leather jacket pulled out a club and attacked her. He then fled.
>
> The journalist, Dana Scarton, said: "Before she could say anything, a guy ran by, crouched down, whacked her on the knee and kept running. Nancy just dropped and started screaming and sobbing. She said: "It hurts. It hurts so bad. I'm so scared."
>
> Frank Carroll, a coach who unknowingly pointed out Ms Kerrigan to her assailant minutes before the attack, said: "How do you get out there after someone's done that to you? How do you concentrate on the triple lutz-double toe loop when you don't know what kind of madman is out there?"
>
> Dr Steven Plomaritis, an orthopedic surgeon who examined her, said there was no fracture, but she had suffered a serious bruise.
>
> Her agent, Mr Jerry Solomon, said Ms Kerrigan had "sustained quite a blow, not only physically but mentally".

2c Who said each of the following?

1 "Why me?" _____

2 'Nancy just dropped and started screaming and sobbing.' _____

3 'How do you get out there after someone's done that to you?' _____

4 '... not only physically but mentally.' _____

3a Read this part of the article about the attack on Nancy Kerrigan and write down the names of the two people who are the main subjects of the text.

> Kathy Stewart, a coach who was at the practice session, said she noticed "a suspicious-looking man" in a black jacket and hat video-taping Ms Kerrigan as she skated. When she left the ice, he followed her, but police have not identified the man as the attacker.
>
> Ms Stewart said the man was wearing official credentials around his neck allowing him to be at the rink. However several witnesses have said they were not asked to show their credentials.
>
> The attack comes just eight months after the tennis player Monica Seles was stabbed by a spectator with a kitchen knife on a court in Hamburg, Germany. She is still recovering from the inch-deep wound and will miss the Australian Open this month. Her assailant, Guenther Parche, was given a two-year suspended sentence. Security has been increased at tennis events since the Seles incident.

The text is mainly about _____ and _____ .

3b What do you learn about what the attacker was wearing that you didn't already know from the paragraphs in 2b?

_____
_____
_____

3c Write down five things you learn from this report about the Monica Seles stabbing which you didn't know before.

_____
_____
_____
_____
_____

It was later discovered that the attack on Nancy Kerrigan had been organised by another skater's husband and bodyguard and they were arrested.

Nancy Kerrigan recovered in time to take part in the Olympics in Norway and won a silver medal in the ladies' figure skating event.

4a In March 1993, there was a nasty moment — in fact a number of nasty moments — at the start of the Grand National, Britain's most famous horse race, which is run at Aintree Racecourse in Liverpool.

Read the headlines and look at the pictures which appeared in some of the Sunday papers next day and choose which of the sentences below best describes what the news was about.

THE MAN WHO FAILED TO WAVE THE FLAG FOR BRITAIN

NATIONAL DISASTER

The race that never was

National ends in fiasco

1 There was no Grand National planned for this year.
2 Something went wrong with the Grand National.
3 A man has been unpatriotic.
4 There has been a major accident in Britain.

4b This is how the *Sunday Telegraph* reported the incident on 4 April, the day after the race. Use the report to answer the questions below.

> The Grand National, Britain's premier steeplechase, was abandoned amid scenes of chaos yesterday, after 31 of 40 horses set off round the Aintree course having failed to notice a second false start signal.
>
> In front of an international television audience, the National, on which more than £75 million of bets had been placed, ended in bewilderment after two false starts. Seven jockeys completed the course, ignoring frantic attempts to halt them.
>
> Last night, an inquiry into the fiasco was centring on a recall, or "flag man", Mr Ken Evans, whose job it is to halt riders after a false start has been signalled. The race was eventually declared void, 50 minutes after its scheduled start, and Aintree officials said the recall flag had not been shown.
>
> However, TV film last night suggested that the starter's flag failed to unfurl after the second false start. Captain Keith Brown, the starter, was booed and jeered as he left the course, at one stage under a police escort.
>
> Mr Evans, a flag man for more than 10 years, was being interviewed by the racing stewards at Aintree last night.

1. How many horses were going to run in the race? _____
2. How many set off, not realising there was a second false start? _____
3. How much money had been bet on the race? _____
4. How many horses completed the course? _____
5. How long after the race should have started was it declared void? _____
6. How long had Mr Evans been a 'flag man'? _____

4c Here is a 'Timetable of Events' which was published in *The Independent* on Sunday, 4 April. Go back to the report in 4a and underline the parts which are listed in this 'Timetable of Events'.

Timetable of events

3.50pm: Animal rights activists invade Aintree, delaying the scheduled start.
3.58: They're off.
3.58: False start immediately declared after starting tape fails to spring up quickly enough, entangling several riders.
4.02: Jockeys re-group at start.
4.03: They're off again. Starting tape fouls again and starter Keith Brown signals second false start, but red recall flag not visible to jockeys, who carry on.
4.04: Only eight realise error immediately, and one shortly afterwards. They return to start.
4.06: Majority of horses still running as race reaches Becher's Brook for first time.
4.09: By halfway stage, more jockeys have begun to realise what has happened and pull out of race.
4.13: Seven jockeys carry on to the end of the race, when stewards' inquiry is announced.
4.32: Stewards still meeting as bewildered jockeys and spectators mill around trying to find out what went wrong.
4.40: Grand National declared void.

4d These words could be used to replace some of the words in the 'Timetable of Events' from *The Independent*. For each one, underline the word it could replace and put the 'new' word in the margin opposite it.

1 demonstrators
2 planned
3 catching
4 mistake
5 soon
6 point
7 investigation
8 confused
9 move
10 invalid

4e Two jockeys were especially upset by what happened. Read what each of them said after the event.

'The tape actually wound round my neck. Horses were treading on it behind me and I nearly got pulled off my horse a couple of times. Whether I wanted to go on or not, I couldn't.'

When we set off the second time, I was up there with the first half dozen. I saw no flag but I did see that something was wrong. I thought it was something to do with the protestors and I carried on. When we crossed the finishing line, I thought I'd won the National.'

4f Read these two paragraphs from another newspaper report and write the name of the jockey who said each of the things in 4e beside his words. Add the name of his horse.

One rider who was never going to travel far was Richard Dunwoody, who found the heavy starting tape winding itself so tightly round his neck that when horses coming behind him trod on the streaming tape he was almost yanked from the saddle of Won't Be Gone Long.

Jockey John White who for a few moments believed he had won the Grand National, was close to tears as he realized that it had all been in vain. 'It's awful!' he remarked. Esha Ness ran well the whole way and now it all means nothing.

4g Why is the name of Richard Dunwoody's horse amusing? _____

_____

In 1994 the Grand National was won by Miinnehoma, ridden by Richard Dunwoody.

Can you think of any other nasty moments in sport?

Has anything horrible happened recently in a sport you follow?

Talk to friends about any incidents you can remember and then list them and the ones described here in order, putting the nastiest one first.

12 The Channel Tunnel

When, in 1802, Napoleon first suggested the building of a tunnel under the channel between England and France, he probably didn't think it would be nearly two hundred years before it actually happened! Eventually, in 1994 his dream was realized and the Channel Tunnel was officially opened on Friday, 6 May 1994 by Queen Elizabeth II of England and President Mitterrand of France.

a 24 hours a day, 365 days a year service

UK Terminal
150 hectares
37.2 km of railtrack
23 km of road
8 loading/unloading platforms

French Terminal
700 hectares
50 km of railtrack
44 km of road
8 loading/unloading platforms

- Special high-speed passenger trains
  - Le Shuttle for cars

- Le Shuttle carries road vehicles from one terminal to the other in 35 minutes
  - Maximum speed: 140 kph
  - Carries coaches as well as cars
  - Special freight shuttles for lorries

- Service for cars, caravans and coaches, every 15 minutes at peak times
  - Over 3,000 passengers an hour
  - At least one departure per hour through the night
  - For lorries, every 20 minutes at peak times when fully operational

- Drive on, drive off
  - Estimated maximum loading time 8 minutes
  - Estimated maximum unloading time 8 minutes

- Two single-track rail tunnels, one for each direction, each 50 km long and 7.6 m in diameter
  - Linked to the service tunnel by cross passages every 375 m

- Eurostar high-speed passenger trains can travel at 160 kph

- Air ducts to prevent pressure build-up

- Non-stop journeys:
  - Paris-London in less than 3 hours
  - London-Brussels just over 3 hours

- Service tunnel – for ventilation, safety and maintenance – 4.8 m in diameter.
  - Can be used to evacuate people in case of fire or accident

- Signs at the terminals and on the shuttles in French and English

1a Use the publicity and information leaflet on the opposite page to answer these travellers' questions. Give them as much relevant information as you can.

1. Can I drive through the tunnel?

2. I don't think I'd like to be in the tunnel for such a long time. What about the fumes?

3. My French isn't very good. How will I know what to do when I get to Calais?

4. Is it open at night?

5. How fast do the passenger trains go? I've heard they're very fast.

6. How long will it take to load and unload Le Shuttle?

7. What happens if there's a fire?

8. Do you take caravans on Le Shuttle?

9. I'd like to stay in Paris tonight. How quickly can I get to London tomorrow morning?

1b What do these adjectives describe in the leaflet on page 66?

1 single-track _____ 3 special _____

2 high-speed _____ 4 non-stop _____

1c Find a place to add each of these words and phrases to the leaflet on page 66. (They are listed in the order in which they might appear.)

Write each one in the appropriate place.

1 in area
2 regular
3 all kinds of
4 just
5 can be carried
6 a shuttle leaves
7 tunnel
8 for example
9 or other emergency
10 both of

2a Look at these 'Key Facts' which appeared in a newspaper article about the Channel Tunnel. Circle any things which you know already from reading the leaflet on page 66.

Key Facts

The cost: Building the Tunnel cost about £10 billion, which is twice as much as was first thought. It also cost ten lives.

The length of the Tunnel: the Tunnel is 50 km long, with 38 km under the seabed of the Channel.

The capacity of a Le Shuttle train: about 120 cars and 12 coaches, and their passengers.

The speed of the Eurostar trains: up to 160 kph

2b Write down:

1 One sad thing about the building of the Tunnel.

_____

2 One interesting thing about the length of the Tunnel.

_____

3 Look at this cross section of the Channel Tunnel and label at least six things. (You will find useful information and words to use in the leaflet on page 66 and in 2a above.)

4a The actual boring of the Tunnel took three and a half years to complete.

Look at this schedule of 'Important Dates' in the construction programme and underline the key words in each statement. (Don't underline more than FOUR words in any one statement.)

2 April 1985	The French and British governments ask for proposals for the design and construction of a 'fixed link' between their two countries.
20 January 1986	A twin-bore rail tunnel, to be built by a company called Transmanche-Link, is chosen as the way forward.
29 July 1987	The necessary formalities for the link are completed (namely the ratification of the treaty).
1 December 1987	Tunnelling under the seabed begins in the UK.
8 February 1988	Tunnelling under the seabed on the French side begins.
28 June 1988	Tunnelling under the land on the French side begins.
30 September 1988	Tunnelling under the land on the English side begins.
21 April 1990	The total length of tunnelling is now 75.7 km – half the total for the complete tunnel.
13 August 1990	The total length of tunnelling now reaches 100 km – two thirds of the total.
1 December 1990	The first breakthrough between the tunnels started from France and from England is made. This is the first time in twelve thousand years that it has been possible to walk between the two countries.
28 June 1991	Tunnelling completed.

4b Find these words in the 'Important Dates' in 4a and give a very brief explanation of each one.

1 proposals for the design and construction

_____

2 fixed link

_____

3 twin-bore

_____

4 necessary formalities

_____

5 the first breakthrough

_____

5 Here are three postcards showing events in the Tunnel as the boring operation got near to completion. Which of the paragraphs below was printed on the back of each postcard?

1 ___

2 ___

3 ___

A Philippe Cozette and Graham Fagg, the workers who won the ballot to break the last wall between the tunnel drives, exchange flags following the breakthrough of the French and UK service tunnels. **December 1990**

B French tunnel workers sign the final tunnel lining ring in the seaward service tunnel, following the completion of the tunnel boring machine's drive. The machine was subsequently dismantled and taken back to Sangatte along the tunnel as scrap metal. **October 1990**

C Through the hole bored to check the alignment of the UK heading, the workers could talk to each other or exchange small items, such as this one franc coin. **November 1990**

6a Read these 'Fascinating Facts' about the Channel Tunnel and:
   – put a tick beside the two which give permission for something.
   – underline the one which you think is most important.

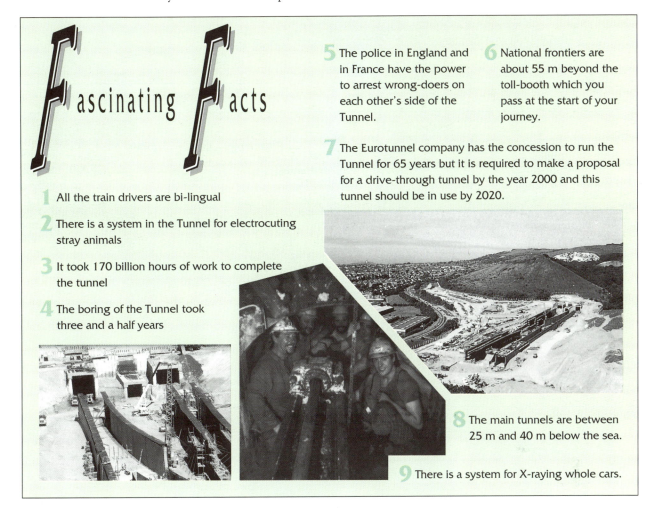

Fascinating Facts

1 All the train drivers are bi-lingual

2 There is a system in the Tunnel for electrocuting stray animals

3 It took 170 billion hours of work to complete the tunnel

4 The boring of the Tunnel took three and a half years

5 The police in England and in France have the power to arrest wrong-doers on each other's side of the Tunnel.

6 National frontiers are about 55 m beyond the toll-booth which you pass at the start of your journey.

7 The Eurotunnel company has the concession to run the Tunnel for 65 years but it is required to make a proposal for a drive-through tunnel by the year 2000 and this tunnel should be in use by 2020.

8 The main tunnels are between 25 m and 40 m below the sea.

9 There is a system for X-raying whole cars.

6b Read through the 'Fascinating Facts' again and put a circle round the key words in each statement. (Don't circle more than FIVE words in any one statement.)

As high as a house and the length of three football pitches.
Look at this photograph. What is it? Why does it say 'One careful owner'? Who might buy it?
Where else might you see 'One careful owner' on a notice?

71

13 Is it a fake?

1a Look at these dictionary definitions. What do the four words have in common?

_____

_____

counterfeit *n. adj.* something made or done in imitation of another thing in order to deceive, e.g. counterfeit money/jewels. *v.* copy/imitate in order to deceive, e.g. coins. **counterfeiter** a person who counterfeits.

fake *n.* something which looks genuine but is not; a person who tries to deceive by claiming falsely to have or be something. *adj.* **fake;** *v.* to make something or pretend to be somebody with the purpose of deceiving other people, e.g. He faked his own suicide.

pirate *n.* a person who uses or reproduces a book, a recording, a film, etc. without authority and for his/her own profit. *adj.* **pirated** e.g. a pirated cassette. *v.* to use or reproduce without authority for one's own profit.

forgery *n.* a copy made of something with the intention of deceiving, e.g. a document / a signature.

1b Can you add five things to this list of items which are often copied and sold as if they are genuine? Come back to your list later and add any more items that you think of.

> cassettes _____ _____
> cameras   _____ _____
> jewellery _____

2a Take a very quick look at these facts about the sale of counterfeit products and write down what product each one is about.

FACT 1 Millions of pairs of fake Levi's jeans have been seized all around the world. Some of the copies look almost exactly the same as the real thing, but the inferior ones often have bad stitching.

FACT 2 Cartier, the makers of expensive watches, suffer enormous problems as a result of counterfeiting. They lose about 10 million US dollars every year from a turnover of about $1 billion. The problem is not the obvious fakes which are sold at about $20 but the near perfect copies which sell for $500 or $600.

FACT 3 Reebok, the sports shoe manufacturers, frequently come across cheap imitations of their trainers. In one month, 1,000 pairs of fake shoes were found in Birmingham, England, and 4,000 more were discovered in Finland. The fakes were good and they were being sold for about two thirds the price of the genuine shoes, so buyers were not suspicious.

FACT 4 In the UK, police seized almost a million pirate videos which had been illegally recorded last year. The quality of most of these copies was very poor. Some of the major film companies are now putting a special security seal on their video cassettes.

2b Use the information from the Facts in 2a and answer these questions.

1 How might you be able to recognise fake jeans?
_____

2 Why is the Cartier company not very worried about fake watches which sell for about $20 each?
_____

3 Why did the buyers of the fake Reeboks in England and Finland think they had got the real thing?
_____

4 What are the big film companies doing to try to reduce the sale of illegally copied video cassettes?
_____

2c Now go carefully through the Facts again and underline all the uses of 'counterfeit', 'fake', and 'pirate' and words which are related to them. In the margin, opposite each one, write down whether the word is used as a noun or an adjective.

3 Read this advice from a consumer magazine on 'How to spot a fake' and complete the chart below.

Bad sewing and poor shape are the most obvious signs that a pair of jeans is a fake. The labels, and how and where they are put on, might also give the game away.

When it comes to audio cassettes, the most usual tell-tale sign is the quality of the recording. Sometimes they have tracks missing or are even completely blank. Quite often, there is a ringing noise in the background which is the result of copying the cassette at too high a speed. Another thing which might help you spot a fake is the quality of the printing on the label.

T-shirt fakes generally have the correct pictures and writing on them (although this isn't always the case!) but often the quality of the printing is awful and the material is horribly cheap.

You probably won't recognise a fake perfume until you get it home. When you try it before you buy it, you will almost certainly be given a sample of the real thing. The bottle you buy will be in a fancy wrapper, so you won't know what you've bought until too late. It's still worth looking at the box, if you have bought the perfume before, as there are occasionally little differences which you might spot.

Whatever you buy, if the price is extraordinarily low, be suspicious!

HOW TO SPOT A FAKE	
ITEM	WHAT TO CHECK BEFORE YOU BUY
jeans	
audio cassettes	
T-shirts	
perfume	

No-one wants to be cheated and to pay high prices for things which are below standard, but there are plenty of people who are happy to buy fakes at low prices, knowing them to be fakes.

4a Read through this newspaper report quite quickly (without worrying about any words you don't know) and find out:

1 when people are likely to buy fakes.

___

2 the kinds of fakes that are popular.

___

Although counterfeit goods are costing companies around the world billions and billions of dollars in lost sales, most people are only too happy to take advantage of the low-price, 'imitation' goods on sale. Although they would never buy a fake watch or a fake Gucchi handbag at home, people change their approach when they travel abroad. They go to street markets and anywhere else where they can seek out the counterfeit 'designer label' clothes and 'Rolex' watches which they know they can buy for a fraction of the price they would have to pay back home.

In fact, bringing home a selection of fake goods is part of the fun of travelling – 'Do you like my 'Rolex'? I got it for fifty dollars!' And the wearing of a 'Lacoste' shirt, even if it is a hideous colour and the crocodile is coming unstuck, is a sign that this person has probably travelled far (although there are few countries now where they are not available!). Many major international manufacturing companies are very concerned because the counterfeit industry now makes up eight to nine per cent of all international trade. No wonder companies and most governments in the world are making serious efforts to stop it. But there are certainly quite a lot of people who hope that that won't happen too soon, so that they can have a bit more fun buying their 'exclusive' perfume, their 'designer' clothes and their 'Rolex' watches first.

4b Read the newspaper report in 4a more carefully and write down:

1 the words in the first paragraph which tell you that people like to buy cheap goods

___

2 the part of the second paragraph which tells you what might be wrong with a fake Lacoste shirt

___

3 the words in the third paragraph which tell you that companies and governments are trying hard to stop the sale of counterfeit goods

___

4 the words in the third paragraph which tell you that many people don't feel that buying counterfeit goods is a serious crime

___

74

4c Find these parts in the report in 4a and answer the questions.

1 '... people change their approach.' Their approach to what?

   _____

2 'Although counterfeit goods are costing ....' Costing what?

   _____

3 'I got it for fifty dollars!' Got what for fifty dollars?

   _____

4 '... there are few countries now where they are not available.' Where what are not available?

   _____

5 '... are making serious efforts to stop it.' To stop what?

   _____

6 'so that they can have a bit more fun ...' So that who can have a bit more fun?

   _____

It may be fun to buy fake watches and illegally copied cassettes may be cheap, but there are some counterfeits that are positively dangerous.

5a Read this article from the educational press. What is it about?

Pharmacists join forces to beat the pill pirates

By Thomas Land

The pharmaceutical industry is combining with the universities, governments and the medical profession in a global campaign to suppress the lethal, $150 billion international trade in counterfeit drugs.

Pill piracy involves production of convincing copies of life-or-death medicines such as insulin, antibiotics and antivirals.

A pharmacy training initiative launched by 20 poor West African countries to confront the growing international trade in counterfeit medicines has been widened into a major United Nations campaign to stamp out a global menace.

The drive involves higher education institutions, the medical profession, drug companies, wholesalers, pharmacists and the packaging industry as well as governments worldwide.

5b Re-write the first paragraph in simple English.

_____
_____
_____
_____
_____

5c What does 'convincing copies' (in the second paragraph in 5a) mean?

_____
_____

5d What has happened to the training programme which was started by 20 West African countries?

_____
_____

5e In the fourth paragraph in 5a, it says that the campaign to stop the sale of counterfeit medicines now involves a number of different groups of people.

What does each group do with medicines?

1 the lecturers and researchers

_____
_____

2 the medical profession

_____
_____

3 the drug companies

_____
_____

4 the wholesalers

_____
_____

5 the pharmacists

_____
_____

6 the packaging industry

_____
_____

76

6 Look at this consumer report about fakes which have been discovered by the pharmaceutical industry. Write down what might happen to people who used these fakes.

We have found some alarming products –	possible consequences of using the product
• bogus malarial tablets which actually consist of nothing but talcum powder	
• fake fertilisers, which contain none of the things needed to feed the soil	
• 'antibiotics' which are made from cheap powders with no medical properties	
• watered down medicines, in which the water causes a dangerous reaction	
• fake insulin, which isn't insulin at all	

Complete this puzzle to find the word in the box.

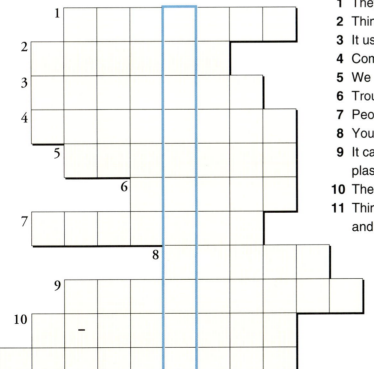

1 They are useful if you have an appointment
2 Things to watch instead of television
3 It usually smells nice
4 Comfortable to wear on your feet
5 We all wear these
6 Trousers made from denim cloth
7 People take these on holiday
8 You can watch them on TV or at the cinema
9 It can be made of gold, silver, glass or plastic
10 These are worn with shorts, but not always
11 Things which can bring us music, pictures and even computer data

77

14 The world of computers

When Charles Babbage developed the first computer in 1830, he could not have imagined the impact computers would have on the world.

1a Look at this chart which shows some of the uses which computers now have. Put a tick (✓) beside any which you have seen in use.

WHERE	BY WHOM	FOR WHAT
shops stores	sales staff office staff	preparing invoices recording what is sold
libraries	librarians readers	for cataloguing books, etc. for finding information
banks	bank staff bank customers	keeping account records, etc. paying in/taking out money
industrial companies	engineers operators	designing new things (e.g. bridges) controlling machines, etc.
ships aeroplanes	navigators	planning and following routes
space vehicles	astronauts	collecting/analysing data from space
business	accountants secretaries	keeping accounts/word-processing, etc.
airlines	reservations staff	making/keeping records of bookings
telephone companies	telephone operators	making automatic connections/ recording the time of calls
publishing companies	designers editors	organising the layout of pages, etc.
tax offices	tax officers	calculating tax, sending out tax bills, etc.
police stations	police men and women	recording and cross-checking details of crimes and criminals

78

1c Use the chart in 1a to help you give short answers to these questions.

1 What do engineers do? _____
2 What do navigators do? _____
3 What do astronauts do? _____
4 What do airline reservations staff do? _____
5 What do tax officers do? _____

2 You almost certainly use computers in your daily life but how good are you at understanding the words people use when they talk about computing?

Some words have accidentally been lost from the screen below.

Choose the correct word from the box to put in front of each definition.

> interface software bit database program
> central processing unit hardware network

_____ comes from 'binary digit'; the basic unit of information in a digital computing system. It can be either 0 or 1

_____ known as the CPU; the part of the computer which does the work by following instructions

_____ a collection of information stored on a disk

_____ all the physical parts which make up the computer system

_____ the communication link between the computer and the operator, or between the computer and another piece of equipment

_____ two or more computers connected together

_____ the set of instructions to be carried out by the computer

_____ the programs used by the computer to perform its tasks

Sometimes, computers don't do exactly as we want them to and seem to 'have a mind of their own'.

3a Read about the computer installed in 1975 by a County Council in England.

The computer was programmed to pay everyone who worked for the Council. Quite soon after it had been set up, it made its first mistake. It paid a school caretaker £75 an hour instead of the 73 pence it should have paid him. Then, it decided not to pay canteen workers at all and none of them got any money for seven weeks! Feeling more generous, it next paid another caretaker £2,600 for one week's work. He realized that the sum was wrong and he sent the cheque back. In a few days he received another cheque – for the same amount. Then, a deputy headmistress was paid her full year's salary regularly every month while school heads of department were paid much less than assistants. And, on another occasion, lots of other people had more money deducted for tax in a week than they earned all year.

Soon, the two hundred and eighty employees decided that they had had enough and they organised a protest meeting. They discovered that only eight people had received the correct pay since the computer had been installed. They all went on strike.

3b Using the information in 3a, complete this report prepared by the person responsible for the Council's new computer.

To: The Chief Executive
From: Michael Robinson
Subject: The computer and the payroll
Date: 4 Feb

I have to report the malfunction of the computer in regard to the payroll. In recent weeks, the following have been underpaid:

_____
_____
_____

Over the same period, the following have been overpaid:

_____
_____
_____

The company which installed the computer has checked the installation and can find no fault.

The software developers assure me that there is nothing wrong with the software.

I have now arranged a meeting with both the installers and the software engineers for next Thursday but a strike has been called for that day.

Please advise me what I should do now.

Michael Robinson

4a Perhaps Michael Robinson should have been advised to call the Disk Doctor.
Read this article about Dave, the Disk Doctor.

Call the Disk Doctor!

Desperate computer users who 'lose' the data from their disks can get in touch with experts who, for a fee, will recover the lost information. One of these experts is Dave Smith, who, some years ago, set up a company called Dave's Disk Doctor Service Ltd. Dave and a few of his friends work from home and give all the money they earn to charity. The fees are always the same, no matter how precious the data on the disk is. Some people, however, are so grateful that they send extra money to Dave or to the charities his company supports. One oil company offered him £1,000 for his help and a vet sent him a blank cheque.

It would be hard to put a value on the things rescued by the Disk Doctor. There have been disks containing medical research, television scripts, manuscripts of whole books, a comedian's joke collection, a solicitor's papers for a court case, and even Margaret Thatcher's itinerary for a visit to eastern Europe. For this last case, Dave was asked if he would go in person to the Thatcher's office 'for security reasons'!

Disks are usually sent to the Disk Doctor by post, but sometimes people are in such a hurry that they can't wait for the post. Radio scripts have had to be rushed by taxi to Dave's house because they were needed for broadcasting the next day, for example. When the material has been recovered, the disk is returned to the sender with a diagnosis and a prescription for avoiding the problem in future. One grateful client, an author, put a 'thank you' to Dave in the front of his book. 'Dave saved me from a cardiac arrest', he wrote. 'But', says Dave, 'most people don't take any notice of the doctor's advice!'

4b Look at the second paragraph of 'Call the Disk Doctor!' List all the things Dave has rescued and write down who would have asked him to recover each one.

medical research – _____   _____

_____   _____

_____   _____

_____   _____

4c Complete these sentences.

1 If Dave had not recovered the medical data, the researcher _____
_____ .

2 If Dave had not recovered the collection of jokes, the _____
_____ .

3 If Dave had not recovered the solicitor's papers, the _____
_____ .

4 If Dave had not recovered the television scripts, the _____
_____ .

5a One person who doesn't seem to need the services of the Disk Doctor is Bob Tomalski, who runs most of his life by computer!

Read about some of the things he has in his home.

Each morning his radio wakes him up with gentle music, the light gradually becomes brighter, the heater switches on and the coffee-percolator begins to make coffee.

For his cat, Bob has provided a warm mat which he can switch on by phoning his home computer system if he thinks it may be a bit cold for the cat while he's out at work. And he's working on an automatic cat feeder!

Needless to say, he has a security system and a video phone as well as lots of TV sets, a mini-cinema and a satellite system, all controlled by computer.

As he comes home from work, he uses his cellular phone to contact the central controller in the house to make sure the percolator is switched on so that he can have coffee as soon as he gets in.

He lives alone with his cat, so he doesn't need the central control to switch off the television or the computer to stop children staying up late or wasting their time when they should be doing their homework!

5b Put a circle round all the things in Bob Tomalski's home which he can operate by computer.

5c When does Bob Tomalski:

1 hear gentle music on his radio?

2 contact his computer to instruct it to warm the cat's mat?

3 use his cellular phone to check that the coffee percolator is switched on?

4 have his first cup of coffee after his journey home from work?

However good you are at using your computer, you might still have trouble with computer viruses. Unfortunately, like viruses which attack human bodies, they can be passed on from computer to computer whenever information is passed between them. Many viruses were designed as jokes, but they have sometimes caused serious problems for computer users.

6a Have you heard of any of these viruses? Tick the ones you know.

1 **Michelangelo** which is supposed to attack computers every year on March 6

2 **CASCADE** which causes letters to fall to the bottom of the screen

3 **AMIGA** which crashes the system and prints 'SOMETHING WONDERFUL HAS HAPPENED! YOUR AMIGA HAS COME ALIVE!'

4 **Fu Man Chu** which searches for the names of political leaders and then replaces them by rude remarks

5 **IBM Xmas Tree** which once displayed Christmas trees on the screen with a Christmas greeting and sent copies to other users of the system. (IBM soon got rid of this virus)

6 **Cookie Monster** which makes the computer stop working and prints '**I want a cookie!**' on the screen. If you type in '**cookie**' the message disappears. The only problem is that each time you type '**cookie**', the faster the message '**I want a cookie!**' returns!

6b Why is the second virus called 'Cascade'?

_____

6c Why do you think the first virus on the list attacks computers on 6 March every year?

_____

Make a list of three things you would like a computer to do for you. Can you think of a way of making one of your ideas possible?

15 Person to person

Dr Ann Lake, a psychiatrist specialising in stress, is planning to go to a medical convention in Tokyo. She has been invited to give a lecture and to demonstrate a new piece of medical equipment used in measuring stress.

1   She needs an import licence to take the equipment into Japan, so she goes to the Import/Export Licensing Office to get one. The woman at the Information Desk tells her she will need form IMP 746.

Can you work out which desk she finally gets it from?

An import licence for Japan? You'll need form IMP 746. Louise will give you one at Desk 8.

INFORMATION (LIZ)

I can only give you form IMP 746, if you've got form LX 14. Karen's got those.

1 MARY

No. I've only got LX 21s. Try Pat on Desk 9.

2 JOHN

I'm sorry I can't help. You'd better go to Information.

3 SARAH

I'm not in charge of any forms at all. Go and see Liz at Information.

4 SUSAN

Sorry, I'm not allowed to give you form IMP 746 unless you have completed form LX 14. You should be able to get that from John behind me or from Desk 14.

5 DAVID

2a Friday will be Ann Lake's last day at work before her trip. Look at her diary for that day.

How many appointments has she got with patients? _____

Friday   16th June

8.30		1.30	Birjees Hassan
9.00	Lucy Bracknell (1st appt.)	2.00	Colin Price
9.30	↓	2.30	Angela Mead
10.00	Sort out post. Dictate letters	3.00	
10.30	Jack Dibley phoning – re. wife Phone Janet Short with title of talk	3.30	REMEMBER to leave keys with Sandra
11.00	Coffee with Dr. Allsopp (from Hilton Hospital)	4.00	n/a
11.30	Philip Cross	4.30	
12.00	Pick Margaret up (asap after 12.10)	5.00	Ben calling for you at home at 4.00 to take you to airport.
12.30	Lunch with Margaret	5.30	
1.00		6.00	

On Thursday evening, just after Sandra, her secretary, has gone home, Ann receives a fax from the Travel Shop.

2b Read the fax and decide how many people mentioned in the diary you think this will affect.

It will probably affect _____ people.

FAX

From: The Travel Shop

To: Dr A. Lake

Re: Your flight to Tokyo

We have just received notification from the airline that the departure time for your flight has been brought forward to 4.00 pm. Please check in by 2.00 pm at the latest.
We regret any inconvenience caused.

2c Ann leaves the following note for Sandra. Read it and decide how many people you NOW think will be affected by the change in Dr Lake's schedule.

I think _____ people will be affected.

> PSYCHIATRY TODAY
>
> Sandra — Thursday evening
>
> My flight has been changed! I've got to be at the airport at 2.00 p.m. Please try and get the three afternoon patients to come in the morning. (It's probably easiest to FAX Angela Mead. I expect she'll want to come as early as possible — if she can make the morning at all. Be careful! A.M. is a very important client.) And I think the best time for Colin Price is probably half past ten. I'll get in early and we'll do the post etc. before I see Lucy Bracknell; then you could try and fit them in betw. 10.00 and 11.30. Let Dr. Allsopp know I can't have coffee with him tomorrow. I'll call Margaret tonight and cancel our lunch. Will you phone Ben please — as early as possible — & see if he can pick me up from here at 12.00.
>
> Ann

2d Look again the appointments in the diary in 2a and put a star (*) beside all the people who Sandra will have to contact.

When Sandra arrives on Friday morning, she begins to rearrange everything.

3a Here is the fax which Angela Mead receives from Sandra. Write in what the missing line probably says.

> DR ANN LAKE, CONSULTANT PSYCHIATRIST
>
> **URGENT**
> **To:** Ms Angela Mead
> **From:** Sandra Frith
> (secretary to Dr A Lake)
>
> Friday, 16 June
>
> Unfortunately, as a result of circumstances beyond her control. Dr Lake has had to change her schedule for today and will be unable to see you at 2.30 as arranged.
> She has asked me to contact you and ask if it might be possible for you
> _____
> appreciate that this is very short notice and, on behalf of Dr Lake, I apologize for inconveniencing you.
> Please fax or phone me with your reply as soon as you can, as I am trying to fit in other patients whose appointments have to be changed.

3b Underline the words in the fax in 3a which show that Sandra was being very polite and apologetic to Angela Mead.

3c Soon, Sandra gets a reply from Angela Mead. Read the reply and write down the time Sandra will now have to allocate to her.

> To: Sandra Frith
> From: Angela Mead   Fri. a.m.
>
> There's a line missing from your FAX. Please re-send.
>
> In any case the only time I can manage today is 11.00. I'll arrive then, unless you tell me otherwise.
>
> A.M.

3d By the time Ann comes in, Sandra has rearranged all the appointments and has told Jack Dibley to phone before nine.

Put all the changes in the diary in 2a.

4 After a hectic day, Ann Lake finally gets to the airport to get the plane to go to Tokyo. Then, she suddenly remembers that she has forgotten to phone Janet Short to tell her the title of her talk for the annual conference later in the year.

She scribbles a fax to Sandra. Read Ann Lake's fax and then complete the fax opposite which Sandra sends to Janet Short.

AIRPORT FAX FACILITY   Fri. p.m. at airport.

Sandra,
  I forgot to phone Janet Short. She'll be furious. She wanted to send the title to the printers today.
  Please contact her first thing on Mon. morning & tell her that my talk should be called "The Effects of Stress on the Memory." And tell her I'll talk to her when I get back (tell her when). And apologise to her please.
       Ann

DR ANN LAKE, CONSULTANT PSYCHIATRIST

URGENT
To: Dr Janet Short
From: Sandra Frith   Monday, 19 June
(secretary to Dr A Lake)

Dr Lake asked me to [1]_____ for not [2]_____ you on
[3]_____ . She was very pressed for time because the [4]_____ was
brought forward and she had to leave [5]_____ . Dr Lake's talk
for the Annual Conference will be [6] '_____ '. Dr Lake
will call you [7]_____ which will be on 4 July.

When Ann Lake finally arrives at the convention in Tokyo, she is horrified to discover that none of the other psychiatrists speak English.

She wants to talk to the Finnish delegate but she can only do so by using the interpreters. Sadly, there is not an interpreter who speaks both English and Finnish. The only thing she can do is to work through a chain of interpreters.

She has to use four interpreters to get her message to the Finnish delegate. Which interpreters does she use?

Dr Lake _____ _____ _____ _____ The Finnish doctor

1
Arabic
Italian
Japanese

2
Arabic
English

3
English
Italian
Polish

4
Finnish
Greek
Hindi

5
Finnish
Portuguese

6
Dutch
Finnish
Spanish

7
German
Japanese
Polish

8
Japanese
Polish
Turkish

9
French
Portuguese

10
Dutch
German

11
English
Turkish

12
French
Greek
Japanese

89

Answer Key

1 What bad luck!

1a 1 a race at the Olympic Games / the Olympic Games 3,000 metres steeplechase
2 Volmari Iso-Hollo
3 in 1932
1b Student's answers will vary.
1c They had to run an extra lap because an official didn't count the laps properly.
1d possible answers:
Para 1 – On target for the record
Para 2 – The incompetent official
Para 3 – The last lap?
Para 4 – An extra lap
1e possible answer:
What a record!
1f possible answers:
excited, confused, angry
The crowd felt excited because Iso-Hollo was on target for the world record.
The crowd felt confused because they were not sure how many laps had been completed.
The crowd felt angry because they thought that there had been a mistake.
1g 1 to run faster than anyone else
2 he was in first place
3 shouted to encourage him
4 was about to start the last lap
2a The words to underline are:
waiting   sure
decided   care
close
2b 1 No
2 Yes, 'he only suffered a broken leg and some bruises'
3 Yes, 'Some people find them hard to get used to.'
4 No
5 Yes, 'where they put his leg in plaster' and 'his hand was put in plaster'
6 Yes, 'the man couldn't hear'
7 No
2c 1 the people at the hospital
2 crutches
3 No problem
4 the neighbour's own house
5 the neighbour's
2d 1 but
2 and
3 as
4 but
2e Student's answers will vary.
Possible answers:
Not you again!
I told you to wait until the ambulance could take you home.
It serves you right. You should have done as I said.
How did this happen?
3a 1 difficulty/delay
2 walk
3 get a free ride by asking for one (from the driver of a car/lorry/etc.)
3b possible answer:
A man got lost in the mountains and tried to hitch a lift
3c 1 Terence Magee
2 an empty chairlift
3 ten hours
3d 1 going down – heading down
2 could not resist – gave in to temptation
3 got on it – jumped aboard
4 shook – juddered
5 hanging – dangling
6 severe – bitter
7 moved from side to side – swayed
8 approaching darkness – gathering dusk
9 shouts – cries
3f 3
3h 1 1.30 am 2 fired a flare 3 get me down
4 chairlift 5 rope ladder 6 throw me a flask with a hot drink in it 7 embarrassed 8 cold
9 lucky 10 zero 11 –6°C

2 What's your favourite colour?

1b Student's answers will vary.
1c 1 blue   5 green
2 yellow   6 purple/violet
3 purple/violet 7 orange
4 orange   8 blue
1d 1 blue   4 green
2 red   5 red
3 purple/violet
1e 1 strength   6 cowardice
2 space   7 depth
3 hope   8 energy
4 holiness   9 sincerity
5 warmth   10 passion
1f 1 orange   4 purple/violet
2 yellow, red   5 green
3 red
1g Student's answers will vary.
2a 1 yellow   4 green
2 pink   5 red
3 red and yellow
2b 1 warm   4 calming
2 calming 5 stressful/cheerful
3 relaxing

2c Student's answers will vary.
3b green, red, yellow, blue, black
3c 1 They also criticise other drivers ...
   2 The research also showed ...
   3 Drivers of yellow cars won't wait in a traffic jam
   4 He is unlikely to get angry with other drivers ...
   5 ... which Henry Ford is supposed to have made ...
3d The following can be underlined (although other sentences could be used too):
   1 It'll probably be green.
   2 And, it is claimed, yellow cars are always in a hurry.
   3 He is unlikely to get angry ... of a side road.
   4 There is a famous remark which Henry Ford '... so long as it's black.'

3 'The Lion'

1a 1 a school magazine
   2 Greylands Secondary School
   3 Barbara Daly
   4 Trips Abroad
   5 twelve (including Contents list)
1b 1 the school's five-year building programme
   2 life without noise and dust
   3 the new rooms and facilities
   4 the school
   5 the exam results
   6 major trophies
1c 1 should be put beside the sentence beginning 'With the recent opening ...'.
   2 should be put beside the sentence beginning 'Where's the window ...'.
     OR 'the chemistry lab was ...' OR 'What's happened to the library?'
   3 should be put beside the sentence beginning 'Exam results were ...'.
     OR 'Our sports teams ...'.
1d 1 Staff Changes
   2 Trips Abroad
   3 Sports Section
   4 Opening of the Mary Bell Music Rooms
   5 Words and Pictures
2a Mr Jessop
   1 September 2 Head of Maths 3 Oxford
   4 Head of Maths at Stratford School
   5 meteorology 6 swimming, walking
   Mrs Howard
   1 January 2 a Chemistry teacher
   3 Edinburgh 4 Chemistry and Biology teacher at New Cross School 5 music (trumpet player)
   6 sailing, music
2b Student's answers will vary.
3b any three from:
   new music rooms
   happy occasion
   eminent violinist
   whole programme
   unforeseen delay
   most enjoyable evening
3c Student's answers will vary.
   possible reasons include:
   car broke down
   lost the way
   made a mistake about the time
   problems at home
   practising for a concert
   (Book 2, Unit 4 tells you that she went to the wrong school.)
4 1 Music Notes
  2 Trips Abroad
  3 Sports Section
  4 News and Comment
  5 School Clubs
  6 Words and Pictures
5a The one on the left was written by a teacher.
   The one on the right by a student.
5b 1 the one on the left
   2 the one on the right
   3 the one on the left
   4 both (The second sentence of the one on the left.
     AND The tone throughout the one on the right is critical as well as the specific 'some fool ran us into the bank').
5c The three sentences to underline are the ones beginning:
   Another wet day!
   It was not funny!
   I'm definitely NOT going to go on any more of Mr. Clarke's adventure holidays!
6b 1 22 (including the title)
   2 because it reminds the reader of the feeling of hating things/to make the feeling stronger
   3 19
6c Student's answers will vary.
6d Student's answers will vary.

4 Agatha Christie's greatest mystery

1b by telephone, by telegraph or by personal call
1c 1 well-built   5 grey
   2 5 ft 7 ins   6 fair
   3 reddish   7 35
   4 hair
1d ... was wearing a green jumper, a green velour hat, a platinum ring with one pearl and probably carrying a black handbag.
2 1 a woman's patent shoe and a woman's scarf should be underlined.
   2 500 should be circled
   3 Newlands Corner should be circled.
   4 at the Colonel's request should be underlined
3a Lots and lots of people are looking for Mrs Christie. People think she is dead.

3b hunt
scour
explored
dragged
combed

4a 1 she'd heard a car earlier 2 a woman of that description stayed there on Friday night
3 quarter past eleven on Saturday morning
4 refused 5 a car going towards Newlands Corner at about 4 am 6 in their lane
7 about 32, well-dressed, with a grey hat on

4b Student's answers will vary.
They could all have been right, but it is unlikely.

5b 1 ... and set down a list of questions and puzzling facts, just as Hercule Poirot might do.
2 Why did Christie drive away from her home in Sunningdale late at night?
3 ... at most an hour's drive from her home?
4 ... where Agatha's husband and Miss Nancy Neele were staying for the week-end with friends?
5 Having abandoned her rather randomly packed travelling case and coat in the car ...
6 ... how did she manage to make the journey to London and then to Harrogate?

5c Yes
that she abandoned her car only an hour's drive from her home
that her husband was staying at a friend's house with another woman, Nancy Neele
that she had taken luggage with her
that she went to Harrogate, via London, and stayed in an expensive hotel
that she bought new clothes
6 Student's answers will vary.
There is no evidence of whether it does or doesn't.

5 Interesting numbers

1 The ancient Egyptians system
I II III IIII IIIII IIIIII IIIIIII IIIIIIII IIIIIIIII ∩
The Babylonian system
v vv vv vv vvv vvv vvvv vvvv vvvvv >
        v vv vv vvv vvv vvvv vvvv
The ancient Greek system
A B Γ Δ E F Z H Θ I
The Mayan system
• •• ••• •••• — —• —•• —••• —•••• ══
The ancient Roman system
I II III IV V VI VII VIII IX X

2b 1 They used the fingers of one hand. Their system is based on five.
2 They used the fingers and thumbs of both hands. Their system is based on ten.
3 They used all their fingers and their toes. Their system is based on twenty.

2c 1 Para 2   3 Para 1
2 Para 3   4 Para 1

3 It is not necessary for the students to try to explain these words in English. Understanding the words, and translating them if they wish, is all that is required.
1 a single number (345 consists of three digits)
2 +
3 −
4 ×
5 ÷
6 put the numbers in the opposite order
7 a list of numbers, with one below another
8 a set of numbers which follow a pattern
9 a regular arrangement of numbers
10 information set out in columns and rows
11 a number multiplied by itself

5a 49   **5b** 111111
4489   222222
444889   333333
44448889   444444

6b 1 by 2 multiply 3 11 4 first
5 multiply 6 by 7 table 8 number
9 table 10 1111 11 1111 12 same
13 multiplied

Challenge!
The first word you get is LESS (i.e. 5537 turned upside down).
(How clearly you see the word depends on the shape of the numbers as they appear on the calculator, so some students will find it easier to see the words than others.)
918 is BIG
7735 is SELL
3705 is SOLE
7108 is BOIL
57738 is BELLS
35007 is LOOSE
379919 is GIGGLE

6 A part-time job

1a Student's answers will vary.
1b Student's answers will vary.
1c Student's answers will vary.
1d 1 a hairdresser's
2 in a house, as a cleaner
   OR in a restaurant/coffee-bar/etc.
3 in a supermarket
4 in a garage/car showroom
5 in a library
6 in an office
7 in a restaurant/coffee-bar
8 in an office

1e 1 part-time   4 minimum 4 hours
2 full-time   5 per week
3 per hour   6 Saturdays

1f phone/tel, apply in writing/write to, call in and ask for

2a No
Hall and Hall ask for someone with good English.

The letter is full of spelling mistakes. He gives very selfish reasons for wanting the job. He's looking for an easy job.

2b The words to be corrected are (in order):
advertisment – advertisement
sollicitor's – solicitor's
shelfs – shelves
photcoppying – photocopying
preffer – prefer
photocoppier – photocopier
wich – which

3a Applicant A is probably the most suitable.

3b Applicant A – if he/she could start work at or after 3 pm
Applicant B – if he/she could be free on Fridays
Applicant C – if he/she could have two weeks off in July

3c 1 solicitor's Applicant A had a summer job in an accountant's office.
2 newspaper Applicant B is the editor of a school magazine.
3 medicine Applicant C is going to study law when he/she leaves school.
4 hates Applicant B loves organising things.
5 was Applicant A wasn't responsible for the filing in his/her previous job.

3d but

4a in a supermarket (or possibly in a canteen or restaurant kitchen)

4b Student's answers will vary.
possible answers:
1 Staff mustn't smoke while on duty.
2 Staff must wear their uniform at all times.
3 Staff must always have carefully trimmed nails.

7 Frankenstein's monster

1 big — enormous
frightening — strong

2b **to be underlined** — **synonym**
decided — made up his mind
the source — the origin
gathered together — collected
unfold — reveal
the deepest mysteries — the biggest secrets
fascinated by — interested in
gradually — little by little
particular — special

2c ... a magnificent superhuman being, about 2.4 metres tall and broad in proportion.

3b The parts that should be underlined in the text in 3a are:
I saw the dull yellow eye of the creature open; it breathed hard, and a convulsive motion agitated its limbs.
His limbs were in proportion, and I had selected his features as beautiful. Beautiful! Great God!
(students may underline the rest of that paragraph).
Unable to endure the aspect of the being I had created, I rushed out of the room.

3c 1 the rain
2 the monster
3 his eyes
4 for the pleasure of creating a living being
5 to make a living creature

4b 1 Justine Moritz, his nursemaid
2 the monster
3 He felt uneasy.

4c 1 because nobody liked him.
2 because he had just saved the man's child from drowning
3 to capture him and try to make him become his friend
4 by holding him by the throat to stop his screaming

4d 1 should go beside 'she was executed'
2 should go beside 'in the mountains'
3 should go beside 'in fact, the father ... afraid of him'
4 should go beside '... in an attempt to silence him ... strangled him'.

5b 1 Yes '... to the jungles of South America ...'
2 Yes '... but knew nothing about what Frankenstein was doing.'
3 No
4 No
5 No
6 Yes '... Frankenstein was searching the inn to make sure the monster was not there ...'

6b 1 He was searching everywhere for the monster,
2 because he was the only 'father' he had had and he had wanted Frankenstein to love him
3 in despair, because he had no friends.

7 Student's answers will vary.
possible answers:
2a A scientific experiment
3a A life is created
4a A fatal embrace
5a More deaths
6a A sad end

8 Well done!

1a The answers are given in the Student's Book, page 47.

1c Student A – 6 marks out of 10
Student B – 8 marks out of 10
Student C – 3 marks out of 10

2 Student A – 16 marks out of 20
Student B – 20 marks out of 20
Student C – 14 marks out of 20

3a Student's answers will vary.

3b The answers are given in the Student's Book, page 47.

93

4 The answers here depend on how the students allocated marks in the previous exercises.
5a Student's answers will vary.
   possible answers:
   Student A: A lovely surprise!
              Your exam result is much better than your term's work. Be careful with spellings – particularly 'they', and with word order in questions.
   Student B: Well done!
              Your answers to Q1 and Q2 are excellent. You should revise the irregular verbs again.
   Student C: A good effort!
              You have obviously learnt the irregular verbs. You should now concentrate on practising prepositions.

9 Staying at the Wessex

1a 1 two other friends, Cathie and Denise
   2 three
   3 the receptionist
   4 £5
   5 £2
1b The answer is given in the student's Book, page 53.
1c 1 at the end of the second paragraph, after 'to unpack'
   2 near the end of the first paragraph, between 'three' and 'beds'
   3 in the last sentence of the text, between 'the' and 'hotel employee'
   4 at the beginning of the second paragraph, after '£30'
   5 Either: at the beginning of the third paragraph, before 'receptionist'
      OR: in the second sentence of the third paragraph before 'colleague'
   6 Either: in the first paragraph, after 'asked for three rooms'
      OR: (but less likely) in the second paragraph, after 'on at present'
2a Shop 2 should be circled.
2b They are (in order):
   Either: They were awfully expensive, weren't they?
   OR: And the sun-hats were just plain white, weren't they?
   OR: The lights were round the window of that shop with the funny salesman, weren't they?
   It was the one which sold black shorts, wasn't it?
   I made a mistake, didn't I?
   And there was lots of swimwear in the window too, wasn't there?
   There were lots of trainers too, weren't there?
2c 1 the shops
   2 one of the shops/the shop which Andy remembered
   3 the sun-hats
   4 black shorts
   5 trainers
2d The sentences to be underlined are:
   I was thinking of buying some.
   They were awfully expensive!
   Sorry!
3a
3b The following should be underlined:
   What on earth has happened to the Wessex lately?
   ... I doubt whether I shall ever stay with you again.
   ... all my shirts were ruined ... compensation
   ... your incompetent receptionist ...
   ... sort out this mess ...
   I do NOT drink alcohol ...
   ... I had to have ... as your chef had not started work.
3c The words to circle are (in order):
   so
   as
   Because
4a

4b 1 ... check it carefully.
2 ... looked at the bill.
3 ... noticed that there were some mistakes on it.
4 ... had tea.
5 ... had a bottle of wine and a glass of brandy.
6 ... had a full English breakfast.

4c The items on Mr Braun's bill should have been on Mr Brown's bill, and vice versa. The receptionist, or maybe other hotel staff, had confused the names Braun and Brown and put the wrong things on the bills.

10 Visitors

1a 'they' refers to the visitors/the relatives
1b 1 the USA
2 with Grandma, in Council Bluffs
3 because she has enough space to have visitors
4 because they are excited
5 Yes
6 because everyone shouts, and they kiss and hug
1d The words to underline are:
costumes, sets, curtains, a part, scene
1e For the writer they are very special and memorable things and she wants to stress them to the reader
1f They fight because Joan always says that everything is better where she lives but her cousin doesn't agree and tells her so
2a The main purpose of each paragraph is:
Para 1 – to describe the room
Para 2 – to tell how Matilda felt about what she saw
Para 3 – to show how kind Miss Honey was
Para 4 – to introduce the idea that there was something mysterious about the house
2b The things to be underlined are:
The room was as small and square and bare as a prison cell.
... a single tiny window ...
... no curtains ...
The only objects ... were two upturned wooden boxes to serve as chairs and a third box between them for a table
... no pictures on the walls, no carpet on the floor, only rough unpolished wooden planks ...
The ceiling was so low ...
It was whitewash ...
2c 1 appalled
2 neat and trimly dressed
3 nice, hot
2d buttered toast, strawberry jam, a piece of sponge-cake
2e because the house was not at all how she expected a teacher's house to be
3a Student's answers will vary.
possible answers:
telephone a member of the family back home in England, if he had any relatives
telephone the immigration authorities, if she had emigrated to the USA
telephone the place where she got married and ask for details from the marriage certificate
3b daugter – daughter
adress – address
sevral – several
Eventully – Eventually
plain – plane
4b Student's answers will vary.
5a It's from a 'fun' book for young people. It is not meant to be taken seriously!
5b Student's answers will vary.
possible answers:
1 ... doing homework.
2 ... on students handing it in on time.
3 ... homework is a waste of time.
4 ... making students do such pointless things?
5 ... 'It's for your own good'.
5c 1 ... peculiar/hard to understand.
2 ... the writer wants to say that it's what parents think is smart, not what is really smart.
3 ... the children ... the parents.
4 ... a threat, but, in fact, the children don't want to go anyway.
5 ... children.
6 ... make them suffer such a boring time that their minds go dead.

11 Nasty moments in sport

1a She was stabbed in the back at an international tennis tournament in Germany.
1c 1 Yes   5 No
2 Yes   6 Yes
3 No   7 Yes
4 No   8 No
1d Number 4 in 1c should be ticked.
1e 1 He was the tournament doctor.
2 He gave her first aid and helped to take her away from the court.
3 They gave her first aid and carried her away on a stretcher.
4 She saw a strange-looking man attack Monica Seles.
5 They pounced on the attacker.
6 They helped the security men.
7 They carried the attacker away.
2a Nancy Kerrigan
She was attacked by someone.
2b A man with a heavy stick hit America's Number 1 figure skater for no apparent reason. She will not be able to take part in the trial event for the Winter Olympics.
2c 1 Nancy Kerrigan
2 Dana Scarton, a journalist
3 Frank Carroll, a coach
4 Jerry Solomon, her agent

3a the attacker and Monica Seles

3b He was wearing a black jacket and hat and had an official badge round his neck.

3c The attacker used a kitchen knife.
The wound was an inch deep.
The attacker's name Guenther Parche.
The attacker was given a two-year suspended sentence.
It took her a long time to recover.

4a 2, something went wrong with the Grand National

4b 1 40   4 7
       2 31   5 50 minutes
       3 more than £75 million   6 10 years

4c The parts to be underlined are:
a second false start signal AND after two false starts
the starter's flag failed to unfurl
Seven jockeys completed the course.
ended in bewilderment
The race was eventually declared void.

4d The words to be underlined are:
  1 activists   6 stage
  2 scheduled   7 inquiry
  3 entangling   8 bewildered
  4 error   9 mill
  5 shortly   10 void

4f Richard Dunwoody Won't Be Gone Long
       John White   Esha Ness

4g Student's answers will vary.
It might be thought amusing because he wasn't gone long! In fact, he hardly left.

12 The Channel Tunnel

1a possible answers:
  1 No, but you can drive your car on to a special train which will take you through.
  2 You won't be in the tunnel very long and there is a good ventilation system.
  3 No problem. All the signs are in French and English.
  4 Yes, it's open 24 hours a day.
  5 The trains can travel up to 160 kph.
  6 It only takes 8 minutes to load or unload.
  7 There's a service tunnel and everyone can get out along there.
  8 Yes, we do, on the car shuttle.
  9 On the passenger train, it takes just under 3 hours.

1b 1 rail tunnels
      2 passenger trains
      3 high-speed passenger trains
      4 journeys

1c 1 after '150 hectares' or after '700 hectares'
      2 before '24 hours a day'
      3 before 'cars'
      4 before '35 minutes'
      5 after '3,000 passengers an hour'
      6 after 'For lorries'
      7 between 'one' and 'for each direction'
      8 before 'Paris–London'
      9 after 'or accident'
     10 between 'Signs at' and 'the terminals'

2a The following things should be circled:
The Tunnel is 50 km long.
up to 160 kph

2b 1 It cost ten lives.
      2 There are 12 km not under the seabed.
      3 The things to label could be:

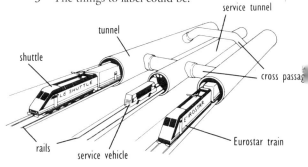

4a The words to underline are:
2 April 1985   proposals for design
20 January 1986   twin-bore rail tunnel
29 July 1987   formalities completed
1 December 1987   Tunnelling seabed UK begins
8 February 1988   Tunnelling seabed French begins
28 June 1988   Tunnelling land French begins
30 September 1988   Tunnelling land English begins
21 April 1990   length now 75.7 km
13 August 1990   length now 100 km
1 December 1990   breakthrough between tunnels
28 June 1991   completed

4b 1 suggestions for what the Tunnel should look like and how it should be built
      2 a permanent/solid connection
      3 two holes
      4 the official arrangements
      5 when the tunnel from France met the tunnel from England

5 1C 2A 3B

6a permission: **5** and **7**
Student's answers will vary.

6b The words to circle are:
  1 train drivers   bi-lingual
  2 system   electrocuting stray animals
  3 170 million hours work
  4 three and a half years
  5 police   arrest   each other's side
  6 National frontiers
  7 Eurotunnel   65 years   drive-through   2020
  8 tunnels   25 m   40 m   below sea
  9 system   X-raying   cars

96

13 Is it a fake?

1a They are all about things people make and do to cheat other people.

1b possible answers:
- videos
- books
- watches
- trainers
- jeans
- T-shirts
- clothes
- handbags

2a
1. Levi's jeans
2. Cartier watches
3. Reebok trainers
4. videos

2b
1. by the bad stitching
2. because they are obvious fakes and therefore not really competition for the real Cartier watches
3. because the quality was good and the price was not much lower than for real Reeboks
4. They are putting special security seals on the cassettes.

2c The words to underline are:
In Fact 1 – fake adjective
In Fact 2 – counterfeiting noun
           fakes noun
In Fact 3 – fake adjective
           fakes noun
In Fact 4 – pirate adjective

3 The answers are (in order):
jeans – sewing; the shape; the labels and where and how they are put on
audio cassettes – quality of recording; missing tracks; recorded/blank; printing on label
T-shirts – writing; quality of printing; material
perfume – the smell (if you can); the box

4a
1. on holiday abroad
2. watches, 'designer' clothes, T-shirts, shoes

4b
1. are only too happy to take advantage of the low price
2. it is a hideous colour and the crocodile is coming unstuck
3. are making serious efforts to stop it
4. so that they can have a bit more fun

4c
1. to buying fake goods
2. billions and billions of dollars
3. the Rolex watch which the tourist has bought
4. Lacoste T-shirts
5. the sale of counterfeit goods
6. the tourists who buy fakes

5a The sale of fake medicines.

5b Pharmaceutical companies all over the world are trying to stop the sale of dangerous counterfeit drugs. They are working with universities and with governments and the medical profession to stop this $150 billion trade.

5c It means that the copies are so good that people don't realize that they have been cheated.

5d It has been taken over by the United Nations.

5e
1. they teach about them and do research into new products
2. they use them/give them to patients
3. they manufacture them
4. they sell them to pharmacies/hospitals/etc.
5. they sell them to the public/to doctors/etc.
6. they pack them in boxes/bottles/etc.

6a possible answers:
1. The patient might die of malaria.
2. The people who use them will have no crops.
3. The illness might continue or get worse.
4. The person might become more ill.
5. The diabetic person might go into a coma and might die.

Challenge

1	W	A	T	C	H	E	S		
2	V	I	D	E	O	S			
3	P	E	R	F	U	M	E		
4	T	R	A	I	N	E	R	S	
5	C	L	O	T	H	E	S		
6		J	E	A	N	S			
7	C	A	M	E	R	A	S		
8				F	I	L	M	S	
9	J	E	W	E	L	L	E	R	Y
10	T	-	S	H	I	R	T	S	
11	C	A	S	S	E	T	T	E	S

14 The world of computers

1a Student's answers will vary.

1c
1. design and construct new things (e.g. bridges), etc.
2. plan and follow routes
3. travel in space and collect data
4. make bookings for travellers
5. calculate and collect tax

2 The answers (in order):
bit   interface
central processing unit   network
database   program
hardware   software

3b underpaid: the canteen workers
                 heads of departments in schools
                 lots of other people
overpaid: two caretakers
            a deputy headmistress

4b medical research – a doctor or other medical researcher
television scripts – television writers / producers
manuscripts of whole books – the authors / publishers
comedian's joke collection – the comedian
a solicitor's papers – the solicitor
Mrs Thatcher's itinerary – her secretary

4c possible answers:
1. ... would have lost all his results.
2. ... comedian would have had to try to remember some or think of some new ones.
3. ... solicitor would have had to prepare the case again.
4. ... the writer would have had to re-write it.

5b The things to be circled are:
his radio   a security system
the light   a video phone
the heater   lots of TV sets
the coffee percolator   a mini cinema
a warm mat   a satellite system

5c 1 when he wakes up in the morning
     2 when he's at work and he thinks it may be a bit cold for the cat
     3 as he comes home from work
     4 as soon as he gets in

6b because the letters falling to the bottom of the screen are like a cascade of water (like a waterfall)

6c It is actually because 6 March 1475 was the date when Michelangelo was born.

15 Person to person

1 She gets the form from Desk 10.
2a 5
2b probably 3
2c 7, including Sandra
2d The people who need a star put beside them in the diary are:
Dr Allsopp
Birjees Hassan
Colin Price
Angela Mead
Ben

3a probably:
... to come at 10.00 in the morning. I ...

3b the words to be underlined are:
Unfortunately
... ask if it might be possible ...
... appreciate that this is very short notice ...
... apologize for inconveniencing you ...

3c 11.00

3d

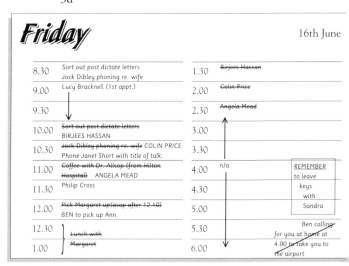

4   1 Apologize to you   2 phoning   3 Friday
    4 time of her flight to Tokyo   5 earlier than expected   6 The Effects of Stress on Memory
    7 when she gets back from Tokyo

Challenge!   The sequence is:
            3 – 7 – 10 – 6